Evolutions of a Law Practice

Evolutions of a Law Practice

How I Opened My Own Practice Right Out of Law School….
and lived to tell about it

Barry Seidel

Cover art by Ryan Urz through 99 Designs

Although this book discusses certain legal issues and principles,
nothing contained in this book should be considered as legal advice. Individuals or entities with legal issues should consult with
appropriate legal counsel of their own choosing.

First Printing, 2019

ISBN 978-1-54398-952-6

Author contact info:

Barry S. Seidel. Esq.
Bseidel@barryseidelassociates.com

www.EvolutionsofaLawPractice.com

Contents

Evolutions of a Law Practice

Why I Wrote This Book

Contrary to much discussion, solo and small firm law practice is not dying. Things are not what they once were for people who want a traditional job in a law firm, though such jobs are still out there too.

While employment prospects have become more difficult for lawyers seeking jobs, law practice opportunities abound, especially for entrepreneurially minded individuals.

I don't know *any* solo or small-firm lawyers who are struggling to find clients. *Good* clients, perhaps, but that's simply a matter of fine-tuning and focus. In reality, if one has a modicum of skill in a particular area of law, there is abundant and growing demand for many kinds of legal services.

And the bottom line is: if one wants to launch and run their own successful practice, it is entirely possible to do so.

I wrote this book to help lawyers and law students who are on their own or are considering that path. I hope my story will encourage people to consider entrepreneurial possibilities, to evaluate their career plans, and to pursue viable career options.

As you'll see, once you've started it's easy enough to bring in business and keep busy. But of course, there are many more business and life considerations.

I hope my story encourages people to discuss such things.

I hope my story helps some people make better decisions and take action if they should.

Pro-actively or re-actively, everyone will have a career path.

Sometimes it's hard to state specific goals, but I hope we can share this one....

WHEN YOU LOOK BACK – HAVE NO REGRETS!

A note on this book's structure: This is essentially a memoir about starting my own solo law practice and the various business and personal evolutions that followed. I've included some real "law stories", though of course I've taken care to change names and details to protect clients' identity and privacy. The stories are all true, and in context for where I was in practice at the time.

Chapter 1

Starting Out

I opened my own law practice right out of law school in 1982. I've never had a traditional lawyer job. Practices evolve over time. Mine is currently in its seventh incarnation. I've made many business and personal decisions along the way. Sometimes change arose reactively—the desire to not be doing *that* anymore—while other moves were more prospective, based on the desire to focus on something new.

When I shifted away from certain areas of the law, the time spent on those fields was never wasted. I always learned, though sometimes not as quickly as I should have. Over time, I've been able to adapt faster, act sooner, and become bolder. Sometimes I made mistakes and then compounded them by hanging on, doubling down in the wrong direction. But, whether through choice or necessity, eventually I always rerouted my efforts and steered where I needed to go.

I graduated from The State University of New York at Stony Brook with a degree in political science in 1978. Like many pre-law students, my thoughts regarding the path to success were linear: go to the best possible law school so I could get the best possible job. It didn't seem too complicated.

Following this strategy led me to the University of Texas Law School. At that point, going to UT Law and living in Austin were the biggest adventures of my life. I enjoyed law school and living in a different culture, but going to law school in Texas was not the usual path to a job back home in New York City.

I suspect most law students only envision themselves as actual attorneys in the abstract, if they think about it at all. Like my classmates at UT and my friends in other law schools, I merely hoped to "get a good job" after graduation. We didn't talk about the day-to-day realities of law practice, just about getting into a good firm and one day making partner. Whatever that meant. To be honest, I didn't know. I listened intently to all this talk and spoke little.

My first inkling of employment challenges ahead came during my second year. Park Avenue and Wall Street firms recruited at UT, and I interviewed with twenty of them. Each interview was like a bad blind date, with an awkward sense of "this isn't going anywhere, is it?" always in the air. I knew where I stood when most never called back.

I did get a second interview with a firm that defended accountant malpractice cases, but even then, I knew there couldn't be enough money for me to spend my days doing that. I also got a call back from a firm doing surety law, but I didn't pursue it because in my mind, it sounded boring. Of course, this really meant I didn't know what it was. Years later, I worked on some cases involving surety law. The field concerns a special kind of insurance (called a "surety bond") designed to make sure someone does what they are supposed to do, and if they don't do it (or do it poorly) a claim could be made against the bond. It's kind of interesting. But back then, I knew best, so I passed.

After my bad interview experiences with the big firms, I figured I'd have to settle for a job at a smaller firm when I graduated. I wasn't discouraged by the rejections. I thought it made sense to get some experience, and I also needed to make a few bucks, so I checked the employment board in the law school's placement office.

I got a part-time job at a small Austin law firm, Milner and Smith. The firm had two partners, three associates, and two law student clerks, plus some support staff.

It was a great place to work and learn. I worked closely with all five lawyers on their projects and assignments. Joe Milner was the principal attorney there. He specialized in matrimonial cases and general civil litigation. At that time, he was in his forties and had been practicing for about fifteen years. I observed that not only was he an expert in his fields of practice, he seemed conversant and interested in many other areas of law.

His associates, who had various levels of experience, were all hard workers. From my perspective they all seemed like fine attorneys. They mostly worked independently, though they frequently consulted with each other and with Joe.

On my first day, Joe gave me my first assignment. (Note – throughout this book all client names are fictitious and facts are varied enough to protect confidentiality; all attorney names are real unless otherwise noted.) Joe wanted me to help his client,

Mrs. Paulson. She was a seventy-year-old woman who Joe had represented in two divorces. According to Joe, she was a decent client who paid her fees on time and in full. He wanted me to solve her present problem, which involved some insurance questions. He wasn't exactly sure what the problems were because she had a speech impediment and he couldn't understand the full story over the phone. In the past he had met with her in her home, but he didn't want to visit if it was not really necessary. He asked me to drive over to her house, see what was going on, straighten out what I could, and keep track of my time so the firm could bill her.

I called Mrs. Paulson, introduced myself, and made the appointment. I got directions from one of the associates and drove to her house.

Mrs. Paulson lived in a small house fifteen miles outside Austin. We sat at her dinette table. She spoke loudly as she showed me stacks of papers. It was a mess; three years of unsubmitted, rejected, or neglected Blue Cross health insurance claims. There were many collection letters from doctors and hospitals, and papers that I thought looked like lawsuits. At that moment the situation needed patience and persistence. I hoped I could sort everything out and communicate some positivity to the client. I knew I couldn't handle all the problems myself, but I knew a law firm should be able to solve the problems.

I brought the papers back to the office, put in some hours, and got the mess organized. Then I discussed the situation with Joe. We determined that some problems were appropriate for me to handle—mostly corresponding with doctors and insurance companies—while the active lawsuits were better suited for the associates.

By the way, no law school class taught me to write letters to doctors and insurance companies. I learned how from Joe's associates. My first few drafts involved a fair amount of trepidation and uncertainly, but I could see that such writing was an essential skill. (see Appendix "A" for my essential guide to letter writing)

The Mrs. Paulson case made me an instant hero at Milner & Smith, mostly because I saved anyone else from having to deal with the most tedious aspects of it. They were paying me $10 per hour, and I saw they billed $100 per hour for my time. I had no problem with that. I was proud when I made money for the firm.

I learned a lot working at Milner & Smith. I helped out on many types of cases. I got to see the business side of things, from how cases were initially evaluated, to how fee arrangements were made, to how back office operations affected the firm.

I was hired at the same time as another UT law student, but we were assigned different kinds of tasks. I noticed the other clerk was mostly assigned matters involving research and document drafting, while I mostly got the jobs requiring travel outside the office. I filed papers in various courthouses, looked up files in court, made house calls to certain clients, served papers, and delivered documents to opposing lawyers. Joe started me on this path right from the beginning, so I guess he thought I had some street smarts. Heck, maybe I did. In any event, there was a lesson in this, which was: If possible, match the right people with the right jobs.

Much of my later office management style and many of my office systems came from lessons learned from Joe Milner. I don't think one could overstate the value in working at a small firm while in law school. Of course, it helps to find a well-run office and to pay attention to more than the individual work assignments. It seems Joe's skills and business acumen have served him well— his firm is still going strong today. See Appendix B (Joe Milner website)

While I learned a great deal working in Austin, I still thought my career should progress toward big New York firms and striving for partnership. So, after two years in Texas, I moved back to New York to attend Fordham Law as a visiting student. I thought it would put me in a better position to pass the New York Bar exam (it did) and get a job in New York (it didn't.)

While attending Fordham I got another part-time job, this time with a solo practitioner named Mark Weingard (this name is fictitious but the stories are true.) Mark was primarily a plaintiff's personal injury lawyer, but he also did an assortment of general practice matters.

Mark's office was in midtown Manhattan. Other than Mark's law suite, the rest of the building was mostly occupied by Indian rug dealers. Mark was in his fifties. He was the landlord over a suite where he rented space to four older solo practitioners.

Mark's tenants ranged in age from seventy-six to ninety. I was twenty-four. I wasn't sure whether they were good lawyers but they sure told great stories. I thought they must have been decent though, since they all seemed prosperous and they were all working and paying rent. One day I realized (this was 1981) that many of those lawyers had been practicing for fifty years, which meant they had started practicing in the 1930s.

One of the offices was occupied by 82-year-old Leo Powell (not his real name.) He was sort of Mark's associate. He didn't have his own clients, he worked for Mark on an "as needed" basis, which was pretty often. His main activity was going to Court on Mark's behalf. I liked when he came back and he and Mark discussed what had happened. Leo was a fierce advocate. Even on small cases, he loved to fight.

My first assignment from Mark was as follows: Mark's client, Jose Ortega, owned a bar which was about to be closed by the Liquor Authority because it was a drug dealing location. Mark brought a court case to stop the bar from being closed while the liquor license matter was pending. My job was to review the hearing transcripts from an earlier proceeding and write something to convince the Liquor Authority to let him keep his license. Unfortunately, undercover agents had recorded many conversations of people asking where they could find "Joe with the good blow". The transcripts showed the bartenders consistently directing the agents to Jose Ortega's back office.

13

I asked Mark how we could possibly overcome this? He said we couldn't, but we had been paid to buy some time to keep the bar open through Christmas.

So, I did my best, Mark submitted what I wrote almost verbatim, and we managed to keep the bar open over the holiday. It ended up being closed just after the New Year. Mark assured me we had done what we were paid to do, and we moved on to other cases.

Mark spoke fluent Spanish and had a large following of mostly Spanish speaking clients. He had a fair volume of accident cases that seemed to be his bread and butter. And, like Joe Milner, he knew about many areas of practice.

I saw him handle purchases and sales of Manhattan restaurants.

I saw him take on all kinds of immigration cases.

He also handled matrimonial cases, sometimes with serious custody and property issues.

He showed me the importance of making referrals to larger firms on certain cases, like medical malpractice and products liability. The key thing, he explained, was to know which firms do not honor referral fee agreements and avoid those firms. He named a few, and I could tell he was speaking from experience.

He also told me which firms were "honorable" and suggested I use them when the situation arose.

I loved working for Mark.

Meanwhile, I was in my third year at Fordham Law School and still going to awkward interviews. I broadened my job search beyond the high end, but nothing happened. It was a tight job market, with no jobs at small or medium sized firms, and no jobs at the District Attorney's office or Legal Aid. Downward employment cycles for lawyers are not unusual.

There were no jobs, but I didn't panic. Instead, while I worked in Mark's office, I kept returning to an idea: "I want to open my own practice."

Now, the plain facts were I had no money, no clients, few contacts, and no clue how to actually open a practice. On the other hand, I knew I had learned a lot from Joe and Mark and their offices and associates. The types of cases they did were interesting, and I could see myself working on similar ones. The thought of being a general practitioner, and knowing about a lot of different things, was appealing.

I met with the Placement Director at Fordham and told her what I was thinking. She said, "It's an unusual idea." Then she added, "Only about three percent of law graduates open their own practice straight out of school, and I've never heard of anyone doing that in New York." She looked down, sorry that she had disappointed me.

But I wasn't disappointed—I stood up and said, "You mean, people actually *do* it?! Three percent! *Are you sure?*"

She replied, "I don't know, I mean I never…hey, wait a minute…" She fumbled around in her desk before she spoke again. "I heard about a book…here's an ad for it, it's by a guy named Singer, and you could probably get it at Strand."

There it was, an ad for "*How to Go Directly into Solo Practice, without Missing a Meal*" by Gerald Singer. To this day, I remember flying out of her office, heading off on a mission, leaving behind a trail of dust.

The book was indeed at Strand, a famous Greenwich Village bookstore. I found it in the back, with its bright blue cover standing out amidst the real law books. I bought the book and started reading it on the subway heading home to Queens. When I looked up, I was five stops past my station. My heart was pounding. This guy's plan, conceived in Los Angeles, could actually work! Not only that, I knew it would work even better in New York City.

I got started that day. My first official act was starting a subscription to the *New York Law Journal*. This is a daily newspaper for New York lawyers. I had seen it in Mark's office; it was not available on newsstands. Besides legal news, it had a huge classified section, with ads for jobs, part-time jobs, office situations and business opportunities. It also listed all the local court rules and upcoming court calendars. I started reading the *Law Journal* every day, and I continue the practice to this day. It keeps you in shape for daily practice. It should be read carefully and with a sense that you may be about to learn something important.

Reading the *Law Journal* every day makes it clear there is a lot to know and always a lot to learn. If law school gets one thinking like a lawyer, reading the *Law Journal* gets one thinking like a *practicing* lawyer. Even reading about unfamiliar areas of law can be valuable, often in unexpected ways.

In the months after buying the book, while still in law school, I began implementing the book's strategies. In a nutshell, the idea was to find a "time for space" arrangement for an office, including referrals of legal work and cases. "Time for space" would include any situation where your rent would be reduced based on some agreed upon work commitment. There were many possible arrangements. An ideal office would be in a building occupied by many lawyers and located near a courthouse.

After securing the time for space with referrals arrangement, you could increase business by meeting other lawyers in the same office and in the building to get legal assignments and referrals. If that didn't get enough work, knock on doors in the rest of the building. Then, send announcements to every person and entity you've known in your whole life. You could also get on some referral panels, do a little advertising, and otherwise think like a businessperson with a valuable product to sell. Add in your own creativity and don't look back.

I asked Mark if he'd let me work part-time once I passed the bar and became a lawyer. Besides the cash flow from working part-time, I knew I'd need his advice when real clients and cases came in. He was on board from the start. I called him when needed, which was not too often. Years later, some of my best professional moments were when he called *me* for advice.

Speaking of part-time work, it is worth noting that if you have a part-time job and ANY private clients, you are, in fact, in practice.

While still in law school and getting organized to start my practice, I saw an ad in the *Law Journal* from a company called Educated & Dedicated. Their ad essentially said, "our clients need a messenger who can go to courts and agencies and figure out what to do when they get there." I knew I could do that, so I contacted them and started getting assignments.

One of their clients was a company called Federal Document Retrieval, who sent me to copy files at various places, mostly the Federal Courts. Their clients were big law firms from all over the country. A frequent assignment was to locate documents at the Federal Archives in Bayonne, New Jersey. Every time I went there was an adventure.

Educated & Dedicated always wanted me to call them with questions, rather than their clients directly. One day I was stuck in Bayonne and couldn't find what their client wanted. Nobody at E&D knew what to do, so I called Federal Document Retrieval directly. Their contact person was Margaret. We got the assignment clarified. Margaret then asked me about my work situation, so I briefly told her my life story, including my plans to open a practice. She asked me to talk to her boss Dave, the owner of Federal Document Retrieval. He got on the phone, had me re-tell my story and then asked, "How would you like to be our exclusive agent in New York?"

And so, I had my first corporate client... a year before my law practice officially started!

Chapter 2

Everything-and-Anything Phase, Especially Landlord-Tenant

I passed the New York Bar Exam on my first shot, and on May 12, 1982 was sworn in as a New York attorney. I thus accomplished every law student's dream, making partner in one day. Now my firm needed an office, and furniture, and telephones, and some paying clients.

I located my first office through a *Law Journal* ad, offering "time for space" with an attorney named Richard Herman (name fictitious.) His office was located within walking distance from Manhattan's Supreme, Civil, Housing, and Surrogate's Courts. Almost every office in the building was occupied by lawyers, law firms, and companies that provided legal services (process servers, investigators, court reporters and the like.)

This was the deal: I paid $100 per month for a furnished office in a suite with other lawyers. My space included a desk, chair, file cabinet, and use of the library, copy machine, refrigerator, and water cooler. Putting my sandwich and juice in that fridge was a real perk.

Richard had many "cases in progress" to refer, and the deal was "work on the cases and split any fees 50/50." This was the "time for space" part of the deal. I was getting cheap rent in exchange for putting in time on Richard's cases.

I soon found out that "cases in progress" were usually cases he'd signed up at various points in history and had done nothing about. Those were the good ones. The bad ones were cases he'd worked on and made worse. I knew which cases to work on first: the ones with a chance to generate some money fairly quickly. Also, cases I had some idea how to do.

Some of these matters just needed a phone call or two, like a five-year-old property damage claim from a car accident. I think the client had forgotten about it and was thrilled when I called with news of his $1,200 settlement. The legal fee for this was $400 (one-third), which should have meant that I earned $200. But it was a little less because Richard wanted $35 in "disbursements," which were expenses he had advanced. I felt funny taking this from the client after a five-year delay, so I paid him out of my share.

This was my first lesson in high finance: never underestimate small-mindedness. Richard had been in practice for forty years and probably had more money than anyone could ever need. But he made toast in his office toaster oven, adding jelly from an unmarked jar. One day I discovered his secret jelly source, when I spotted him scooping little packets of diner jelly into his private stock.

In Richard's six-office law suite, each office was occupied by a different solo practitioner. I introduced myself to all the lawyers in the suite, and all the rest of the lawyers on the floor. I didn't make a schedule or a detailed plan for this networking, it just happened. Every lawyer had work for me. Some gave outright case referrals, but they mostly sent me on court appearances on civil cases. Since I had never been to court as a lawyer before, this was on-the-job-training.

Many of Richard's cases were salvageable, and despite his idiosyncrasies, working with him helped me along. Some of his clients called me directly on new matters. He wouldn't have missed them and considering the nature of his practice, I never felt badly working directly with these clients.

Besides Richard's cases, and the appearances and referrals from the other lawyers, I had some additional business building ideas. I sent 500 announcements to a list of friends, acquaintances, relatives, and people my mother suggested.

You might be surprised that people are willing to hire an inexperienced lawyer. Based on my many years as a clientologist, I now understand the psychology of this seeming folly:

People want a lawyer who is affordable (a skeptic would say "cheap") and has time to give their case attention. That's IT. If you are a lawyer, people assume you know what to do. Most of the time you *do* know what to do, but even if you don't, you know you can easily learn.

The announcements generated some decent work: I got some collection cases from a college classmate's business partner, a deathbed will for my cousin's friend (which soon turned into an estate), an uncontested divorce referred by my family doctor, and a steady stream of other cases.

Some of the lawyers in Richard's suite sent me to appear for them in Manhattan Housing Court. Each time I went there, I witnessed hundreds of people doing the same mad dance hour after hour. The dancers were the lawyers and court clerks and judges. The clients, both landlords and tenants, didn't dance much. They mostly screamed at each other.

I got assignments on all kinds of Housing Court cases. The lawyers knew I didn't know much, so they told me all the scenarios for their particular situation and how to handle each one. I was a quick study, so pretty soon I knew what to do and how to act for many kinds of appearances.

In Housing Court I noticed something about court systems. When there are more cases than any courthouse could possibly resolve, something must be done to finish the cases. That something is providing both sides with an incentive to settle.

In Housing Court every case gets a conference. Both sides are given options they don't like. If both sides agree to be unhappy and reach a compromise, you have a stipulation of settlement (a "stip") and the Court is happy. One of the things court personnel are always yelling is "Any stips? Why don't you just stip? C'mon, stip and you can get outta here!"

If one side or the other doesn't want to stip, the parties are told that something bad will probably happen. For a landlord, the case could be adjourned month after month while the tenant lives rent-free, and when the case finally comes up for trial the case might be dismissed because the papers are technically "defective." The landlord might then be told, "Off the record, you shoulda stipped to give the tenant three months free in exchange for his leaving. Now you have to start your case over."

Tenants got hammered too. If they didn't stip as suggested they might get an immediate trial, where they'd likely lose and then be evicted.

I saw both scenarios many times.

There were two kinds of lawyers in Housing Court. One group were the "irregulars." They were always screaming at their clients, screaming on the phone, or doing a mumble-stumble shuffle all morning. They were undoubtedly general practitioners who were there for one case.

By contrast, the "regulars" had volume. They floated above, gliding from room to room. They spent their mornings like short order cooks, checking in everywhere, conferencing cases to get their stips working, checking back for the status every so often, and then picking up the finished stips before lunch. After lunch they were winning trials against the "irregular" attorneys and the *pro-se* (self-represented) litigants.

I thought Housing Court cases had potential as an area of focus for my law practice, mostly because I couldn't imagine experienced lawyers choosing to do it. Since Richard's suitemates were sending me to Housing Court anyway, I decided to grow my practice by focusing on Landlord-Tenant cases.

I tried a few different strategies to get started in the L&T game:

Whenever I met other lawyers, I asked them for Housing Court appearances and referrals. This included irregulars I met in Housing Court.

I took a class at the New York County Lawyers Association on Landlord-Tenant law. It cost $75. At the class I met some experienced L&T lawyers and judges, and obtained many useful forms and templates. As an aside, back then Continuing Legal Ed (CLE) was not mandatory. But then, as now, there's always value in any class where you learn useful things.

After taking the class, I put an ad in the Manhattan Yellow Pages. At that time (1983) lawyer advertising was new, and just becoming acceptable. The ad cost $6 per month with a 12-month commitment. This was an introductory offer for a listing under "Landlord-Tenant Lawyers." I was pretty sure there would be competition (I mean, it was Manhattan!), but I also figured I would be available and ready, and for $6 a month ($72 for the first year) how could it lose? My entire financial analysis was, "If I got one case I would break even, anything additional would be profit."

When the Yellow Pages came out there were only five lawyers listed in Manhattan in the Landlord-Tenant section!

It is very gratifying when an advertising idea works and the phone rings. I got calls almost every day. To my surprise, many of those calls were from landlords. You might think landlords have lawyers on retainer. While big landlords often do, most smaller landlords don't.

You might think landlords would not resort to the yellow pages and retain a neophyte lawyer. You might be generally correct, but one great thing about New York City is that even a small percentage of a large group (New York landlords) is a lot of people. Some of those early cases turned into nice fees and others weren't so big but at least yielded cash flow, valuable experience, and crazy stories.

One of my Yellow Pages calls turned into one of the wildest situations I've ever been in. I probably got some business and life lessons out of it as well.......

First Real Law Story: Over My Head and Landing on My Feet (names in this story are all fictitious, all events described actually happened)

Mike and Sharon Stern called about a tenant problem. They owned a ten-unit building and lived in one of the apartments themselves. They also owned a retail store, worked long hours, and managed the building themselves. If the building were a candy store, it would feel nice to call it a Mom & Pop store. A Mom & Pop apartment building doesn't feel as nice.

One of their tenants, Tommy Bazillo, had a rent-stabilized lease but had been legally subletting the apartment for the past two years. As far as the Stern's knew, he had an apartment someplace else and was gone. The subtenant asked for a lease, but they refused to give her one. They were legally correct; they didn't have to. They wanted to rent the apartment to a doctor friend, Jerry Marks, at a higher rent. Two days before the end of his written lease, Tommy Bazillo knocked on Mike and Sharon's door and said "I'm back in the apartment. Under the law you have to keep giving me renewal leases, and I want that, unless you want to make it worth my while to leave."

Sharon and Mike told Tommy he did not have renewal rights and they knew he had another apartment. Mike escorted him to the street, while Sharon went into the apartment, made a list of the very sparse items inside, and placed the items in the basement for safe keeping. Mike then changed the apartment door lock.

Three weeks went by and the Sterns heard nothing from Tommy, so they rented the apartment to Dr. Marks. He promptly commenced $30,000 worth of renovations.

A month later the Sterns were served with legal papers from Tommy's lawyers, for a date in Housing Court. Mike also got papers for Criminal Court, charging illegal eviction, a misdemeanor. The Sterns did what any experienced landlord would do, they got out the yellow pages and called ME.

Not wanting to meet a big landlord in my little office, I offered to visit them at home, for which they were most appreciative. After hearing the facts, I told them it seemed like the tenant was trying to shake them down for a settlement, and the Housing Court realities indicated they should make a small offer, considering the number of court appearances it might take, with their busy schedules and all, and the legal fees that might accrue. Kicking and screaming they authorized me to appear in court and offer the tenant as high as $1,000.

Tommy's lawyer had filed an Order to Show Cause, so essentially the Sterns had to show the court why Tommy shouldn't be put back into possession or awarded money. On the court date I put my Housing Court training into use and requested a conference, certain it would result in a negotiation and then a stip, if not immediately, on a future date.

Tommy's lawyer was willing to talk, but her attitude and demeanor were disconcerting. She was a short, serious woman in her mid-thirties. I could tell she meant business. We went out into the crowded hall. "Can you put my client back into possession?" she asked.

"No," I answered, thinking about the Dr. Mark's renovations.

She responded, "Okay, $75,000 then."

I said, "What are you talking about"?

She replied, "Look, you seem like a nice guy, but our firm specializes in illegal eviction cases. The laws have recently changed and this case is a sure winner. Changing the locks without going to Court first is a big no-no under the new law. Why don't we adjourn this a week and you can look up the things I'm telling you about?"

I took a breath and said, "Even if this is technically a wrongful eviction under the new law, how can you be making a claim for $75,000?"

She shot back, "Tenants in rent stabilized apartments have automatic renewal rights. He pays $650 a month now, but the market rent for this West Village apartment is $1,500. Now, take the difference and factor in his life expectancy. He's twenty-seven years old. Also, the new law provides for treble damages and attorney's fees."

Ouch!

So, we adjourned for a week. I went to the library. She was correct, the wrongful eviction law had changed six months earlier. This was not a nuisance case, it was serious.

I went to visit the Sterns, who were not happy. They were mostly furious at Tommy, and sure he had set them up. If they were upset at me for not initially understanding the situation, they didn't say.

I concealed my nervousness while my mind raced. An idea hit me, and I said to the Sterns, "Let me see your insurance policies on this building."

Until that moment it hadn't occurred to me, but I had seen something in the *Law Journal* about insurance coverage for unusual claims. Although it was written in obscure language, the Sterns' insurance policy had a section on wrongful eviction lawsuits. I wasn't 100% sure on first reading, but there was something in there about it.

I sat in the Sterns' living room and studied the policy. Before too long I was convinced they had insurance for this type of case. I told the Sterns I would call them in a few days, after I notified their insurance company and saw their response.

Back at my office I called Mark, who said I had to formally notify the insurance company (which I already knew) and that I should document all my activities.

To get the insurance coverage rolling, I delivered all the paperwork to the insurance company (they were two blocks from my office), with a cover letter demanding that they take over the defense, and otherwise insure the Sterns in the Housing Court case of "Tommy Bazillo vs Mike and Sharon Stern."

Two days later I received a telegram (in 1983 faxes and email had not yet been invented) from the insurance company disclaiming coverage and refusing to defend the Sterns.

I was pretty sure they were wrong. From my law office experiences I knew that situations like this are why we have courts.

I wasn't sure exactly what to do after the insurance company disclaimed, so I called Mark again.

He said, "You have to bring a D.J. action."

"A what?"

"A lawsuit in Supreme Court for a Declaratory Judgment (D.J.), asking the Supreme Court to order the insurance company to do what they are supposed to do: come into Housing Court and defend your clients."

"Oh, okay. Got any forms I can use?"

He had something basic he'd once used in a trip and fall case. Not exactly on point, but a start. This was going to take some work, and some time.

I showed up in Housing Court on the next court date and told Tommy's lawyer "Listen, we have insurance, but the company disclaimed and I have to file a D.J. action, so you should give me an adjournment. I can't talk settlement with you because it would blow my DJ action. How long can you give me?"

She nodded and smiled at me, in subtle recognition that I was making a smart move that was in both our best interests. We agreed on a two-week adjournment.

Two weeks turned out not to be enough time to finish the D.J. case, so we actually started a trial in Housing Court. Fortunately, Dr. Marks showed up in Court and told the Judge he was the current occupant of the apartment, and although he was not named in any papers or served with any legal notices, he had come into court because he heard someone was trying to get his apartment.

Truth be told, he initially came over to me in the hall and told me all those things and asked if I was representing him! I explained that I wasn't and I couldn't, but suggested it would be helpful if he told the Judge what he had just told me. So he did.

The Judge must have been upset with Tommy's lawyers for not giving me a longer adjournment, because he ordered an immediate hearing (called a "traverse") to see if Dr. Marks was a proper party (he was) and whether the lawsuit papers had been properly served on him (they weren't). So, in the middle of the trial the Judge declared a mistrial. When I updated Mark later that day, he said he never heard of a mistrial in Housing Court. But who cared, I now had some time. Tommy's lawyers would have to start their case over, and of course they did.

Meanwhile, I filed the D.J. papers in Supreme Court, basically an Order to Show Cause (with supporting papers from my client and from me) where the insurance company would have to show cause why they didn't have to defend the Housing Court case. I served the Order to Show Cause on the insurance company and waited for their opposing papers, but they never came. When I appeared in Supreme Court on the hearing date of my DJ action, I was sure the insurance company would ask for time to oppose me, but they didn't show up. My papers were submitted to the

Court without opposition. This made me nervous. I called the insurance company lawyers and asked, "Are my papers so weak that you don't think the Court will order you to defend and insure the Sterns?"

"Not at all," came the reply. "We know you are right, there *is* coverage. We just don't think there is any exposure to monetary damages. So, we'll let it run its course."

I was ready for this. "Excuse me, but are you aware of the new law? And rent stabilization versus market rents? And treble damages plus legal fees? Read my papers, your policy says you must cover for damages where the landlord is legally responsible. The claimant is twenty-seven years old and they are claiming a rent differential for his life expectancy. Plus attorney's fees! You have a lot of exposure here!!"

"Hold on," he said. Fifteen minutes later he came back on. "When is the next Housing Court date?"

"Day after tomorrow. 111 Centre Street, 9:30 AM, Ninth Floor, Judge Bramsen."

"We'll have a money man there." *Click.*

Bottom line: they sent a representative to Housing Court and we negotiated a settlement where the insurance company paid Tommy and his lawyers $22,500 and the Sterns were off the hook.

After settling in Housing Court, Tommy never showed up in Criminal Court. But I went there and told the DA and the Criminal Court Judge what had transpired in Housing Court, and the criminal charges were dismissed.

One small detail remained. Insurance companies are not only supposed to insure, their coverage includes paying lawyers for defense of legal cases. I had done the work they should have been doing. I called and told them this.

They asked for an hourly statement.

Not having kept time sheets as I went along, I had to reconstruct my time, and probably lost some hours. It still came out to eighty-four hours. I used an hourly rate of $75 per hour (at that point I didn't really have an hourly rate, but this seemed low enough that they wouldn't dispute it.) My bill came out to $6,300. The insurance company received my bill and one of the supervisors called, saying, "We all looked bad on this one, but the bill is too high, can we talk about it?"

"The bill is right and fair."

"We think some of the hours you listed are prior to when you notified us."

"How many hours is that?"

"Hmm, about four."

"What do you want to do then?"

"Cut the bill down to $6,000 even."

I thought about this for a few seconds, and said, "I'll agree, on one condition... have the check ready so I can come pick it up right now."

"Okay."

And that was that.

I might add that the Sterns became my clients on many other matters over a 35 year period. Years later I asked them whether they realized I was just starting out and had initially underestimated the case. They said they did, but they also thought I was the kind of person who would figure out what to do. Which is nice.

Landlord-Tenant cases got me into the thick of "lawyering."

However, even though I was getting pretty good at L&T, I didn't want to become a "regular" with a high-volume L&T practice. I knew this would take a full-time commitment and force me to exclude other areas of practice. I can't say I disliked L&T, but I did not want to BE an L&T lawyer.

Chapter 3

Landlord-Tenant Evolves Into Real Estate

I stayed at my first office for two years, from 1982 to 1984. I did my own typing and answered my own phone. I had an answering machine where I called in for messages. I carried change and called in often, from phone booths in court and on the street.

Even though I wasn't making as much money as my peers with jobs at big firms, I was making a living and running my own business. I was aware of my net income relative to my home expenses. We lived a modest but totally comfortable lifestyle. While I didn't have a monetary definition for "success", I acknowledged that money WAS part of the equation. I just wasn't there, yet. When I heard some of my friends were making "lateral moves" and working with headhunters to move up to better jobs, I was happy for them but not the least envious. I was quietly glad not to be involved in such things. My practice would go where I decided to take it.

In 1984, I started thinking about moving my office closer to where I lived. Commuting from Queens to Manhattan by subway was draining and seemed like a waste of time and money. I also liked the idea of developing a neighborhood practice.

I saw a *Law Journal* ad for a space in a suite in Forest Hills, Queens.

Charles Knox LaSister III, (this time the name is real), an attorney who was a few years older than me, had a lease on the whole suite, which consisted of his spacious corner office (second floor wrap-around overlooking Austin Street and Continental Avenue in Forest Hills), three smaller offices, and a conference room. Knox carried himself with an air of confidence and success, in a way that caused me to like and respect him.

He had two other lawyer "tenants," though it seemed like most of their work came from him. At that point I wasn't really looking for referrals from the other lawyers. I learned a lot from Knox, more business than law, the most important lesson being to pay attention to the business opportunities in the combination of business and law. My rent ($400/month) included electric, use of a library, copy machine, fridge, phone system, and receptionist. The office was about 5 minutes from where I lived.

At that point I had a variety of cases, and proudly said I had a "general practice." Besides Landlord-Tenant cases, I had some divorces, some small business transactions, some wills and estates, some accident cases, and some minor criminal cases. I answered the "what do you do" question honestly, by saying I was in general practice, with a focus on landlord-tenant cases. I liked L&T cases for what they'd given me: courtroom experience, client experience, and income. But I liked general practice, and learning new practice areas, even more.

Still, while general practice can be appealing, it has some real disadvantages. These mostly come into focus when confronting adversaries who specialize. Over time, as more and more lawyers narrowed their focus and specialized, this became an ongoing problem.

As a generalist, you can't know the law as well as specialists. You can't know the judges and court personnel as well as they do. You can't have an office staff with skills comparable to the specialist's staff. You won't have every form readily available.

In some practice areas, especially when specialists have volume, it's also hard to be price competitive with them. Even worse, when you have other types of cases, you can't afford to get stuck in court on one complicated case. This is especially bad when your adversary has volume (and is in court anyway) and doesn't care if you wait around. Those are money losing situations.

Even with my L&T focus, I was finding ways to be a generalist and expand my lawyering skills. I was always conscious though, that everyone should focus on SOMETHING.

In the mid-1980s, there was a big development in the New York City housing market. Landlords were converting thousands of rental apartments to co-op ownership. Essentially, tenants were given the opportunity to buy their rental apartments at an insider price. This created all kinds of legal activity.

At one point, I answered a *Law Journal* ad for a part-time position (yes – I answered interesting classified ads even when I was established in practice). A landlord firm was bringing "non-prime residence" cases against tenants. They were looking for ways to evict certain tenants, so the landlord could sell their apartments on the open market and not have to sell to the tenant at the insider price. My job would have been to gather enough evidence to evict the tenants or drag them into court and try to buy out their interest at a discount. Pretty awful stuff, so I passed on the job.

But it got me thinking. Many tenants were going to buy their apartments, and they would need lawyers. There would be contracts, and bank financing, and closings, and all the stuff that usually goes with a real estate transaction.

If you asked most lawyers, "what kind of case is a co-op purchase?" they'd say, "real estate", because it involves contracts, and bank financing, and closings. When I looked in the Yellow Pages lawyer ads in the real estate section, I saw many ads for co-op conversions.

It struck me though, that most potential clients (renters who were about to become apartment owners) considered this a landlord-tenant matter, because they were dealing with their Landlord about their apartment. I looked at my Yellow Pages ad in the L&T section of "Lawyer Ads," and noticed that none of the other ads mentioned co-op conversions.

I called my Yellow Pages rep and asked whether I could keep my ad in the L&T section, but make reference to co-op conversions. He said "Yes, and you can also have up to five words with your ad, for $60 per month." I did some math and thought "That's $720 per year. I would need one or two co-op clients to break even. Anything above that would be profit." So, I placed an ad in the L&T section of the Manhattan and Queens Yellow Pages with my name and the added words "Co-ops, condos, contracts and closings".

When the book came out, I was the only lawyer listed that way in the Manhattan and Queens Yellow Pages.

The phone rang with new clients every day.

I took a Continuing Legal Ed course and learned the basics of co-op transactions. It wasn't that hard and I learned something new on every deal. Sometimes the adversary lawyers were the best teachers. When the lawyers were receptive to it, I asked a lot of questions. Their main objective was to get the deal closed smoothly. Teaching me how to get it done was in their best interest.

I also realized that many of my friends and family (and their friends and family) were buying their apartments. The constant young lawyer question ("What do you do?") became much easier to answer. My new ready response was, "General practice, with a lot of co-op and condo closings."

Some tenants were taking buy-out money and buying houses. Or, they were buying their apartments at the insider price, and when market prices rose, selling the apartments and buying houses. I was turning down the house closings because I didn't know enough to fake it. Learning actual real estate law felt like too big an undertaking, especially when I was busy with co-ops and general practice,

One day though, a title insurance salesman walked into my Forest Hills office. He asked who my title company was, and I told him I didn't have one because I didn't do house closings. He asked why not, and I told the truth, "I don't know how to do them." He said, "Well, I'm not a lawyer, but the owner of the title company is a lawyer, and I'm sure he would teach you to do it, in the hopes you would become a customer."

And so, on my first ten house closings, Larry Litwack of Big Apple Abstract told me what to do. When the seller's attorney sent me a proposed contract, Larry and I reviewed it together. I soon learned what a lawyer needed to know about real estate. I became a steady customer for Big Apple Abstract. Not only that, over the years I referred them other attorneys who ended up bringing them even more business than I did. They ended up getting some great results from a cold call and an offer to help a young attorney.

I bolstered my real estate knowledge with some CLE classes, including a free seminar from a rival title company. I learned a few things, got some useful forms, and gave them a title or two. The Yellow Pages ads continued to work well for co-ops, and I soon adjusted my ad to feature house closings too.

Besides co-op and house closings work from the Yellow Pages, I grew the real estate practice by making myself known to local real estate brokers. Brokers will refer you deals, with their primary concern being that you get contracts out fast, don't kill too many deals, and don't charge so much that clients change their mind about selling.

Of course, you always have to find the right balance between doing what the brokers want and keeping your ethical obligations to the clients. That balance being quite simple: *always* put the clients' interests first; and act accordingly. At the same time, it makes sense to do things fast and responsively for the brokers, and make sure they know it. If they don't understand that sometimes you may have to kill a deal as a lawyer for your client, let them torture some other attorney.

Focusing on real estate closings allowed me to increase my income. It was my main practice area for about five years, but I started to see some problems with real estate practice.

Closings were on a flat fee basis, which can be a problem when you can't (or don't) control the time spent. It used to bug me when a married couple were buying a house, and after the husband called and asked a lot of questions, the wife would call and ask all the same questions. Yes, there are solutions to such problems, but it took me awhile to figure that out.

Ultimately, flat fees are bad business, unless you are accomplished enough to raise the fees, or have enough volume to hire paralegals to do most of the work. I considered these measures but did not see enough upside to justify trying either approach. And, financial projections for a real estate practice often assume the real estate market will stay at high levels of activity. In reality, of course, sometimes the market slumps. When it does, it directly impacts a real estate practice. Real estate downturns generally happen right after you hire a new person to help handle your increasing volume. I know this because it happened!

By the late Eighties the co-op conversion frenzy had begun to subside. It made sense to expand my practice beyond real estate.

I also had some personal matters to consider.

Shortly after starting my law practice, Felicia and I were married. We had been together since college. Her entrepreneur's approach supported my solo practice aspirations. By the late 80's we had some serious new challenges, including having a daughter with special needs. This involved a substantial commitment of time, energy and emotion.

Taking on personal challenges is not that different from business, except the stakes are much higher. You have to identify problems, consider options, make decisions, take actions, and make adjustments. We did all those things, repeatedly. When I think about our journey with our special daughter, as amazed as I am about her accomplishments, and what we put into it, it is also amazing that through it all the law practice marched on!

At that point I liked real estate work but didn't love it. I thought it had limitations, which could be overcome but it was not going to be by me. The prospect of working really hard and simply making a living was discouraging. For the first time, earnings started to really matter, and I decided I wanted to "make some real money." I didn't define what this meant, nor did I state an actual target. It was a sense more than anything else, but it was very much in my thinking.

41

The only practice area where I could see potential for "real money" was negligence (accident) cases.

Chapter 4

Negligence Cases a/k/a Trying To Hit Home Runs and Eat Better

I learned the basics of negligence cases when I worked for Mark. I knew enough to handle basic car accidents, and I always had a few cases without having actively sought them out. In the Eighties and into the Nineties, you could settle most auto cases without putting in an overwhelming amount of work.

Some cases, like when someone falls on a property, are a little more complicated. When I got one of those, I asked around and figured out what to do.

Make no mistake, the specialized negligence lawyers have methods, skills, and resources generalists often don't have:

- They invest money in investigation, expert witnesses, and trial prep.
- They develop a skilled support staff to keep the cases moving efficiently.
- They have relationships with doctors who know how to document a case and are prepared to testify at trial.
- They have referral sources feeding them viable cases.
- They are not intimidated by major cases. The insurance companies know which lawyers know how to prepare and try a big case, and which ones don't. When it comes time

for a case to settle, the settlements often reflect the status of the plaintiff's attorney.

- They are up on changes in the law, which occur often.

As I waded into the negligence world, I didn't have these things in place, but figured I would develop them over time. In the back of my mind, I hoped to become a trial lawyer too.

I did have some marketing ideas for negligence practice.

My first move was placing classified ads in out-of-state bar journals. I thought of this after noticing out-of-state attorneys advertising in the *New York Law Journal*. Since they ran the ads month after month, I figured they must be working.

At the time I had a law student working for me. I asked her to write to the bar associations of the other forty-nine states, plus Puerto Rico, and get their monthly journals and advertising rates. We both looked through the stack of bar journals. Pretty interesting stuff. They all had classified sections and published between eight to twelve times per year. The classified rates varied, but none were overly expensive.

The first states I tried were Connecticut, Pennsylvania, Illinois, Texas, and California. I skipped New Jersey and Florida because a lot of New York attorneys were already advertising there, and the rates were high compared to the others.

My ad said, "New York attorney available for referrals of personal injury cases in metropolitan NYC area." It had my name and phone number. That was the whole ad. The monthly ad charges were between forty to eighty dollars per month, per state. I made a little budget, and figured that for those five States, at an average of sixty dollars per month per state, it would cost three hundred dollars a month. If I tried it for six months and nothing happened, I would be out eighteen hundred dollars. It was worth a shot.

I got a few calls from the ads in Connecticut, Illinois, Texas, and California, but they didn't amount to much. Pennsylvania, on the other hand, got me into the negligence game.

The Pennsylvania Bar Journal ad cost forty-two dollars a month. No other New York lawyers were advertising there. A week after the ad went in, an attorney from Pittsburgh referred me a pedestrian knockdown where his client was hit by a car in downtown Brooklyn and broke her leg. The vehicle had a $100,000 insurance policy. Six months later I settled that case for $90,000 without filing suit. I made a $30,000 fee. The Pennsylvania lawyer didn't even want a referral fee. That case alone paid for the Pennsylvania ad for the next 877 years.

I then got a call from a negligence lawyer in Philadelphia who was advertising on cable TV, using an 800 number. At that time, 800 numbers and ads on cable were relatively new. Some of his ads were on TBS in Atlanta, but the station was being picked up in other markets. He was getting calls from potential clients in New York and wanted to refer the cases to a New York lawyer. It seemed like a low risk offer with lots of upside, so I agreed to receive the referrals.

Some of the cases were really low-end and I rejected them. The Philadelphia attorney said he'd be fine with that, and he was true to his word. However, many of the cases were pretty darn good. In the negligence world, "good" means someone got hurt pretty badly and there was a legally viable claim to be made against a defendant who has insurance. This is the basic analysis for how lawyers decide whether to accept contingency fee cases, which is an essential element of negligence practice. It's a series of ongoing and repeated business decisions. See Appendix 3 for discussion of the contingency tripod (legal liability, serious injury, collectability.)

The Pennsylvania ad, and my Philadelphia connection in particular, brought in a steady stream of new cases. I stopped running the other state ads and stuck with Pennsylvania. The calls and new cases were worth the $42/month.

I also contacted local doctors and chiropractors regarding accident case referrals. I found they were amenable to working with a young personal injury attorney. They all understood they should treat liberally and build up the cases. I would be referring them cases where they could treat the patients and be paid by no-fault insurance. I figured some of the doctors would have patients who came in directly and needed a lawyer. All it took to get some referrals from the doctors was asking.

Back then one could handle soft-tissue cases profitably. (Note – in the negligence world bone fractures are objective: you can see them on an x-ray and show this to a jury. Soft tissue cases are more subjective, so when the person says something hurts, a jury may or may not believe them. To a person with a bona-fide soft tissue injury, the injury hurts and is real. Nevertheless, the value is harder to establish than with a fracture. All in all, soft tissue injuries are generally considered to be lesser cases).

Back then most insurance companies were willing to settle soft-tissue cases relatively early in the process. Over time though, many insurance companies began vigorously defending such cases and forcing the plaintiffs to press on through the Court system. This must have proven a good strategy for them, as they've maintained this approach for many years.

So, although soft-tissue cases became less desirable over time, back then it was good business, and I vigorously sought more.

Another thing I did was market my practice to other negligence attorneys. Marketing to competitors may seem counter-intuitive, but I never saw it that way. I was looking for referrals. One type of referral were cases that were too small for bigger firms to handle, but big enough where they could receive a referral fee from me. I paid attention for opportunities to do this.

I also sought out conflict of interest situations -- usually driver-passenger cases where a passenger had a claim against his host driver and the other car's driver, and at the same time the host vehicle driver had his own claim against the other car. This creates a potential conflict of interest between the host driver and his passenger (who usually know each other), so the situation requires additional, independent counsel.

I also sought referrals for cases venued in Queens. The location of a case is called "venue", and there are rules for where one can venue a case. When I could legally venue a case in Queens, I did. But I also knew that many plaintiff's lawyers, especially those in Manhattan, didn't prefer Queens cases. There were a few reasons for this:

- It was not as favorable a County for jury verdicts as the Bronx or Brooklyn (though far better than Westchester or Nassau County). This is mostly a function of the jury pools, but to be sure, deciding where to file suit is a fundamental question in every negligence case.

- For most lawyers, going to the Queens County courthouses was difficult and inconvenient.

- For some reason the Queens courts had a lot of quirky rules and practices that were not used in other places. Not knowing the local rules and customs makes most lawyers nervous.

I was frequently in the Queens Courthouse on my own cases, so I began to identify myself in the negligence world as "the Queens guy." Some Manhattan and Long Island negligence lawyers really responded to this. Once again, a small percentage out of a big pool had a real impact.

At one point a negligence lawyer with a nice practice retired and decided to refer out his remaining cases by county. I thought that was a pretty smart approach, especially when he referred me thirty Queens cases at once. It was a mixed bag: a few good ones, a few middling, and the rest low end. That was alright by me. The good ones hit for some nice fees, and the rest were workable.

A few lawyers hired me just to handle portions of their Queens cases. These were mostly depositions, but sometimes court appearances in the Jamaica, Queens courthouse. They knew I was there anyway, so they paid me small fees to do some easy appearances.

All in all, my various marketing efforts brought in plenty of business.

I'm not saying this to brag, but to emphasize that when you market, your marketing WILL work. However, your *practice* will only work if you are ready to effectively handle the work you generate. You should be ready for the marketing to succeed and be prepared to efficiently handle an increasing volume of cases.

Don't be someone who says, "that would be a good problem to have." You don't have to spend a fortune building an infrastructure in advance. But you should be learning about the available technology for managing volume and be ready to implement systems.

To handle the volume of negligence cases, I became an early user of the SAGA software. In the Nineties this was a cutting-edge system for accident case file management and document production. I hired a secretary/paralegal who was a SAGA expert. She knew way more about back office negligence practice than I did. Hiring her was expensive, but well worth it. I was able to handle a case volume that I could not have managed with lesser support.

I got the negligence practice cooking pretty well. I still did some real estate and general litigation too, but 80% of my income was coming from the accident cases. My net income was up about 25%. So, I was eating better, but the increased income was not otherwise transformative.

Negligence cases are great when they settle, but managing volume is a challenge. You have to energetically sign up new cases (before someone else does), deal with clients, run the back office, keep the documents and discovery moving, go to depositions and settlement conferences, and be ready to try a case now and then.

Being a negligence lawyer accomplished my weakly stated goal of making more money, but the 25% income increase did not make me feel successful or happy. Instead, I felt unrelenting pressure to keep the cases moving.

In addition to the challenge of managing the workflow, I felt personally conflicted about the nature of personal injury work. It's strange; the vast majority of negligence lawyers I knew were honest and hard-working. I respected them, but even so I cringed when people referred to "ambulance chasers."

Looking back, I cared about such things way too much. I should have resolved my insecurities or adjusted my path. But I didn't.

Self-image wasn't the only problem. The repetitiveness of the cases wore on me. After a while, the car accidents and "slip and falls" all seemed the same. For most clients the whole case came down to "How much money will I get and when?" I can't say I blamed them for this, but it just left me feeling empty. Even when I had clients who had sympathetic cases, people who were badly hurt and whose lives would never be the same, I was rarely enthused.

As I continued marketing and working, I started to regularly express my disdain for the work. It was a backhanded way of telling the world "I'm not really doing this." But of course, I had decided to do it and WAS doing it! It seems ridiculous now, but that was my mindset.

I also realized that I was missing the opportunity to become a respected trial lawyer. I was encouraged by the positive feedback I received on the few trials I did. Clients, adversaries, jurors and judges seemed to regard me as an effective advocate. But I knew I hadn't tried heavy injury cases to verdict. The reality was, given the scope of my practice and the time commitments to run it, it was impossible to advance my trial skills by doing big trials.

I've watched top negligence lawyers try big cases to a jury. The best ones share a common trait. They speak to juries in plain words while subtly encouraging the jury to feel their client's pain and want to compensate them monetarily. I thought I could do this. However, working alone and managing a high volume of cases, all on a tight budget, always made it too risky to go all the way to trial.

What often happened was the cases would get close to trial and the insurance company offer would go up a bit. At that stage trying the case involves investing money to have doctors testify in court, plus gambling with the client's possible settlement money and gambling on my fee. After all, if you try the case to a jury verdict, it is possible you (and the client) could get nothing, or way less than the offer on the table.

One option was/is to give a third of the fee to an outside trial lawyer (which I did sometimes), but then the final number would have to go way up for it to make sense. The financial realities of trials were stiff challenges to face down, and created incentives to close cases out by holding on as long as possible and then settling. Which was mostly what I did.

Part of me wished I could gamble and experience the risk and thrill of rejecting a settlement offer, rolling the dice to seek a big jury verdict.

I don't regret avoiding the gambles though. I never sold a client short and I never risked a client's financial future by gambling on a trial when I shouldn't have.

Law Story: Watching Harvey Weitz Sum Up

I liked watching how top trial lawyers worked. Some were flashy and bombastic. Some were plain spoken and mild tempered. No matter what, they always succeeded at bringing across that they authentically, down to their cores, believed in their client's case.

Of course, downplaying the dramatics works best when you have a compelling set of facts and devastating injuries that speak for themselves. One day I was in Brooklyn Supreme Court and had just settled one of my smaller cases. As I was leaving the building I saw Paul Weitz, a young attorney who had just started working for his father's firm, Schneider, Kleinick, & Weitz. I knew him a little from another case, so I said hello. He said, "My Dad is about to sum up on a big case upstairs. If you have time you should check it out." So I did.

Harvey Weitz was well known and in his prime as a top trial attorney. I had met him a few times. He was very friendly and down to earth. Up to that point, I had never seen him in action.

In personal injury cases, the plaintiff opens first at the start of the trial and speaks to the jury last during summation. When Paul and I walked into the courtroom, a lawyer for the City of New York was about to start his summation. I noticed that the jurors were looking at him quizzically and the judge was barely listening. The City lawyer's summation was essentially this: "We acknowledge that there are serious injuries and we do not deny that the plaintiff is entitled to compensation. We also know that Mr. Weitz is going to appeal to your emotional side. We are relying on you to do what is fair. As you know, your job is to determine an amount of money that would be appropriate compensation, and in this case I suggest to you that one million dollars is a fair and proper amount." I thought to myself, "If they're conceding one million dollars, the injuries must be pretty bad."

When Harvey Weitz got up to speak, the judge stopped reading and moved his chair closer to the jury box. He was paying rapt attention, as were the jurors. Harvey started talking about things that regular people do in their regular lives. He took his time and talked about mundane things.... Making coffee, eating breakfast with your family, getting dressed, going outside..... He then handed the jurors pictures of the plaintiff in his present condition. I couldn't see the pictures, but I knew what they must have been. Harvey stopped talking for a few moments, and I noticed that every juror was crying. Not one or two, every last one of them.

I didn't stay for the verdict, but a week later I read in the *Law Journal* that a Brooklyn jury had awarded a $26 million verdict in a case against the City. Cases with huge jury verdicts are usually settled while appeals are pending and the amounts are reduced somewhat, but still, millions get paid to the injured party and the lawyers.

I knew what the main skills were: straight talk, integrity and the ability to tell a story. Some evidence rules and medical knowledge would need to be learned, but nothing overwhelming.

But I also knew that the only way to become a real trial lawyer was to regularly try cases. One way to do this would have been as an associate at a firm, working alongside top lawyers. Another way would have been to work at a smaller firm and have them just throw me into the trial action. I knew some excellent trial lawyers who learned just that way.

I came to realize this was a possible drawback in my "right out of school" practice model. When I jumped into the game without having learned trial skills on someone else's dime, I couldn't learn it while I was grinding out my living. It would have been too expensive and risky.

That being said, negligence lawyers can effectively hedge their bets, and make good fees, without doing the trials themselves. One way is to develop working relationships with top trial lawyers. Besides their coming in towards the end to try the case, they can help your prep from the beginning. You essentially ask them "What should I do now to enable you to try this case optimally when the time comes?" If they end up trying the case and making a piece of the fee, so be it. More often though, that better prepped case will settle for you at a better number.

Another way to make serious money in the negligence world (and in law practice generally) is to make outright referrals on major injury cases, especially malpractice cases. This is one of the best and most cost-effective moves one can make in practice.

These are truly win-win-win situations. If you put some thought and effort into the referral, the client wins by getting the best possible lawyer for their particular case. The lawyer who receives the referral wins by increasing their client base with a case they would not otherwise have had (and by receiving a vetted case with a client already favorably disposed toward working with them.) And you, the referring attorney, win by making a fee on a case where someone else does the heavy lifting.

The rules regarding referral fees vary from State to State. The standard is generally not difficult to meet. In New York, for example, the referring lawyer has to maintain shared responsibility for the case, the total fee cannot be more than it would otherwise have been for the client, and the client has to be aware of the fee sharing.

Over the years, even before I focused on negligence cases, most of my best fees were on cases I referred out.

High-end trial lawyers know how to work up cases for maximum value. Investigation and experts are expensive, but when the insurance companies know the plaintiff's lawyers have spent it and are prepared to spend more (and force the insurance company to do the same), and they are facing a lawyer at trial who has a strong track record, settlement values go way up.

The value goes up even more when the case goes all the way to verdict. It's worth noting that civil cases are often settled *during* trial, and sometimes even while the jury is deliberating. Going to verdict is a gamble for plaintiffs, but it forces the insurance company to gamble too. When they know the plaintiff's trial lawyer can "ring the bell," (and they know this because big verdicts are reported in journals and known in the industry) they often opt not to gamble by raising their offer and settling the case. Such settlements are substantially higher than pre-trial settlements.

So, when I am contacted about a case involving serious injuries or death, I do a detailed evaluation. For specialties like medical malpractice cases, I've learned enough to thoroughly evaluate cases for possible referral. If I think a client has a viable case, I work hard to become the referring attorney, advocate for the client to the specialist attorney(s) and protect my referral fee. I learned this last lesson the hard way, but thankfully I only had to learn it once.

If I think a case has some upside value, I will contact multiple firms on the clients' behalf. If the claim is unusual or specialized, I will research for firms to refer to. Some clients can do this on their own, but many can't. Helping a client find the best lawyer for their case is the right thing to do. And, it's worth it.

To any attorneys who scoff at making referrals, I say this: You're nuts!

I learned some other lessons while building up my personal injury/negligence practice. Here are a few:

Sometimes negligence attorneys are presented with shortcuts for getting new cases. These invariably involve paying "investigators" or "runners" to bring in cases. If you are in the game, or new to the game, and this possibility is presented to you, I offer this simple advice: *Don't do it!*

Sometimes the people offering their services are legitimate and professional investigators. They know how to take photos, get witness statements and records, and actually help prepare the case. Investigators are useful to negligence attorneys. You should use one, but only to investigate and prep your cases. If you have a lead on a good case, use a good investigator. However, if an investigator offers to bring you cases they signed up "in blank," as in, they signed it up and now want you to be the attorney: *Don't do it!*

This case forwarding activity was rampant when I was in the negligence game. I knew this because many times when I had a previous client who was in the hospital after an accident, they reported that while in the hospital they were besieged by hospital personnel and other "visitors" trying to steer them to particular lawyers. Every so often there are stings and scandals and arrests about this kind of thing. You may meet people who offer to send you cases this way, for a flat fee or a percentage of your percentage. *Don't do it!*

I also heard about people who had "contacts" at insurance companies and could help get a claim resolved (for a fee). This may not be as widespread as it once was, as many persons of this ilk are now in jail. That being said, if you are approached with something like this, *don't do it!*

I realize I didn't have to actually tell you all this, but things like this do come up, so be aware.

In the negligence world, some plaintiff's attorneys were very direct about suggesting ways for clients to add value to their cases. Additional medical treatments and procedures (especially surgery) add value, as does delaying a return to work. I realize this could be considered part of advising the client, and this type of advice was what many clients wanted. Sometimes, after I explained all this to the client, they'd say, "I would rather go back to work sooner, and as far as having more procedures or surgery to add value to the case, that's just crazy."

In hindsight, I was naïve when I jumped into the negligence world. But I had my eyes open and paid attention. Personal injury claims are a multi-billion dollar industry, with players on both the plaintiff and defense (insurance) side. There are also many related support businesses (medical treatment and exams and testimony, court reporting, technical support, and more). Representing clients requires knowing the players and playing the game well.

Despite my mixed feelings about negligence practice, I learned more about life and business being a personal injury attorney than anything else before or since

Chapter 5

Per-diem Biz …. "Bad is Good"

While I sometimes felt satisfaction in getting a measure of justice for injured people, and while the fees for negligence cases were better than the fees for closings, the cash flow was sporadic. Cases have to be settling or no money comes in.

Another challenge in negligence practice is the day to day workings of the court system. It can be maddening. I would spend entire mornings in Court waiting to do various "conferences". They are called conferences, but mostly you just fill out forms that schedule "discovery", which is providing medical authorizations and records, scheduling depositions, and scheduling medical examinations by the insurance company doctors. The New York court system manages its overwhelming case volume by scheduling many conferences at the same time, so lawyers spend a great deal of time waiting around.

The system suits insurance companies defending a volume of cases. They can assign a few lawyers to stay in one location and do the conferences, but for solos and small firms, waiting around for these brief appearances is a waste of time. As a solo negligence lawyer, traveling to various courthouses for these appearances was a real problem.

Since I venued most of my cases in Queens County, I was most familiar with the Queens courts. Sometimes there was no legal basis to venue a case in Queens, so I filed in whatever other County was best. This resulted in my having quite a few Bronx and Brooklyn cases.

Most cases involve numerous court appearances, many of which are essentially ministerial. They don't require huge skill, but they have to be done right and they require a court appearance.

I had cases in seven other relatively close counties (Bronx, Brooklyn, New York, Staten Island, Nassau, Suffolk, and Westchester). New York practice is like that. When I traveled to courts outside Queens, there were always annoying problems. Even minor things like traffic or subway delays, or having to remember the particular rules in each county, were stressful.

When I had appearances outside Queens, I didn't know the judges or clerks or adversaries or local customs. Then, when I got back to my office, I'd be worn out and tired. In every court I noticed a few lawyers, mostly insurance guys "moonlighting," making appearances for other lawyers. I asked around and learned they charged $75 - $150 per appearance. I would have gladly paid someone $75 to go to Brooklyn for something easy like a preliminary conference.

When I was in the Queens courts, I often had more than one appearance on my own cases. I knew how everything worked. I noticed how hard it was for the non-Queens lawyers to be there. It had all the things I hated about other courts...bad parking, annoying rules, huge volume, and lots of waiting around. I started wondering whether other lawyers would pay *me* to make appearances for them in Queens.

I got out a yellow pad and did some math. It seemed possible to make five to ten appearances per day, in one building. At an average of $100 per appearance this would be $500 - $1000 per day.

There was another possibility I liked: the clients for this work would be other attorneys. As nice as many of my personal injury clients were, I grew tired of having to explain the negligence game again and again. If I were making appearance for other attorneys, they would be my clients, and of course they already knew the game. The thought of having attorneys as clients was very appealing.

At that time making such appearances existed, but it was not widespread.

I knew how the moonlighting insurance lawyers got appearances. They networked with their existing attorney contacts and used word of mouth with other lawyers in court. I started doing that and got a few appearances. Occasionally I saw ads in legal newspapers for "court appearances." I answered some ads and placed some ads and got a few more appearances.

I then made another marketing move that really worked!

This was in 1995. The court system had just started computerizing. There was one publicly available computer in the Queens Courthouse. I looked in the *Law Journal* for cases where a "Request for Preliminary Conference" had just been filed. Using the case names and index numbers listed in the *Law Journal*, I sent my law student clerk to the court computer with instructions to make a list of plaintiff's attorneys with newly filed PC requests. I figured that if I could get PC appearances, I'd probably also get the later appearances (motions, compliance conferences, depositions, pre-trial conferences) too.

Once we had the list, I wrote a cover letter to get across the following points:

- I am in practice, so I understand what you want in an appearance.
- I am in the Queens Courthouses every day, so I know how things work there.
- Making appearances in the Queens courts is a problem I can solve for you.
- My services are reasonably priced, so trying me out should be an easy decision.

I also created a special Rolodex card. Back then every lawyer, but more importantly every calendar clerk and secretary, used a rolodex. My rolodex card had my contact info, but more importantly, while my name and contact info were on the body of the card, the tab said simply "Queens Court Appearances." I wanted them to file my card in their rolodex under "Queens." See Appendix D.

I priced the PC's at $75 and other court appearances at $100. I included my cover letter, price list, and rolodex card in all my mailings. During a six-month period I sent the mailing to 1350 law firms. These were all firms who had just filed for a PC in Queens County. Those mailings yielded 175 new law firm clients for Queens Court appearances! I was on to something.

Many of the lawyers told me my letter came at just the right time. Some told me that Queens was a tough courthouse, so they were happy to know about and use my service. After doing a PC for them, most of the firms started using me for later appearances on the same case and on all their other Queens cases. Many told their lawyer friends, who then used me too.

The mailing got me very busy with court appearances. I had to develop systems to efficiently intake and prep and bill and collect on all the work. Now, I'm no tech genius. Felicia (my wife) is not a tech genius (or a lawyer) either but was way more tech savvy than me. We discussed the workflow for court appearances: managing the intake of assignments, setting up each assignment for court, reporting the results, tracking outsourced appearances, billing, and collecting. We (she) then customized Quickbooks (a widely used accounting software) for the court appearance business.

In Quickbooks lingo, the law firms are my "customers" and the cases I cover are the "jobs." When setting up for court I use the "estimates" feature in Quickbooks. We called this a "pre-bill" and used it as the cover sheet for the assignment and whatever papers the lawyers sent me.

I decided to print the pre-bills on pink paper so I could quickly locate them in Court. This helped keep things organized while handling a high volume of appearances. We referred to the pre-bills as "pink sheets" and the job set-up as "pinking it up." The pink sheets were great for marketing because lawyers in Court noticed the pink sheets and asked me about it. Whenever they asked, I told them what I was doing and gave them a rolodex card.

In our system, when an appearance is done, we convert the estimate into a report and invoice (a standard Quickbooks function) and send it (back then I mailed, later we mostly emailed) to the law firm client. The invoices then post to a Quickbooks ledger for each attorney/customer, so I can follow up on payments. We also made drop-down menus with all the different types of appearances and all the judges. We streamlined the set-up and reporting and billing as much as possible.

Some days it was so busy I sub-contracted appearances to other attorneys. It seemed like attorneys willing to do this kind of work had suddenly materialized. I had to figure out how to price the payments to the other attorneys, so I did. I had to figure out how to keep track of subcontracted work. So I did. For the subs we made another drop-down menu. I had to keep track of who had done what and pay them. Quickbooks calls such people "sales reps", but we changed the name on the pink sheets to "covering attorneys". Sometimes the appearances were in two different Queens buildings. This arose when I landed a few high-volume clients in the lower level local court, Queens Civil Court. The Civil Court cases were mostly collection cases on behalf of high-volume collection firms. If the firms were some distance from Queens, and many were because they had cases all over New York State, my service was a good fit.

Civil Court was in a different building. I developed a system for handling cases in two buildings. I had my new law clerk (a night law student who looked like a grown-up) answer the calendar and mark my cases ready in Civil Court and then conference with the defendants (who were usually *pro-se*, i.e. no attorney) until I arrived from Supreme Court to finish the job. I disclosed this to the Judge in Civil Court, who agreed to let us do this as long as we did not delay the calendar. This was rarely a problem, and I think he cut me some slack because he respected that I disclosed it rather than hiding it, and he saw I was hustling. It also helped that we treated the *pro-se* litigants respectfully and settled a lot of cases.

Things were going great guns. I built the per-diem business up to fifteen to twenty appearances per day, sometimes more, and the business was growing steadily. I had my law student in Civil Court gaining skills and handling volume.

I found a reliable attorney to whom I could sub-contract many of the Supreme Court appearances. This was Diana Gianturco, who was building her own Queens court appearances practice. She saw what I saw, that this business worked, and was better in many ways than private practice with regular clients. Although we were technically competitors, neither of us treated things that way.

There was a big demand for the service and not many people set up to do it. We were each building a service business where there was plenty of work and we both needed help. So we helped each other. She had a growing following, but at that time I was probably her biggest client. I was subbing about 25% of my appearances to her. We agreed on a volume discount and prompt payment and it worked.

We started calling what we were doing "per-diem appearances." That's right, Diana and I coined the phrase!

All kinds of crazy things happened as attorneys (and the court system) saw what we were doing.

One example: In the late Nineties, the judge in the Trial Assignment Part ("TAP") was the renowned Justice Alfred Lerner. There was a huge volume of cases in Queens TAP. They were there for "pre-trial conferences." If cases could not be settled, they would either be adjourned for a further conference or a trial. If a case had previously been marked "FINAL", and it didn't settle, it could be assigned for jury selection that day and then go right to trial. The exact sequence of events was up to the TAP Judge. Judge Lerner rarely did trials himself, that was not his role. His role was to find a way to resolve cases. He was skillful at applying pressure to encourage (some would say force) settlements. One of his techniques, after he could not settle the case at an initial conference, was to have the lawyers report to court every day for "jury selection." There was a jury selection clerk who supervised a series of jury selection rooms, but Judge Lerner controlled who actually got a room and selected a jury. Once lawyers were sent "to select," Judge Lerner had the jury clerk hold them in court every day until 3:30 PM, then send them home and have them come back day after day. Sometimes this went on for weeks. Very often the lawyers adjusted their settlement posture and after a few wasted days sitting around, the case would be settled.

Diana and I started offering a jury selection "monitoring service," though among ourselves we called it "babysitting." Judge Lerner wasn't too happy that we were solving this problem for the plaintiff's attorneys (and by the way, the whole jury selection thing wasn't a problem for the defense attorneys because most of them billed for it).

At one point, Judge Lerner started directing Diana and I to "start picking." Of course, these were not our cases. We were there as per-diems doing babysitting! We called our lawyer clients and told them what was going on and then went in the rooms and started picking a jury. The firms would usually get someone there to take over in a few hours or the next morning.

Some firms didn't bail us out right away, so we even started a few trials and then settled, and also recruited some young trial attorneys who were willing to jump into these emergency situations.

This insanity went on for a few months, culminating in a case where I did a conference in TAP on a case called "Rodriguez v Singh." The case didn't settle, so it got sent for jury selection. We babysat the case for a few days (along with about five others). On the third day the jury clerk put me in a room on a different case and said Judge Lerner had directed me to start picking. He then said Rodriguez v Singh also had to start jury selection immediately or it would be dismissed.

I ran up to TAP and told Diana what was happening. We went to a phone booth and called the plaintiff's attorney. He freaked out at first, but then realized he had to focus and ask what his options were. We said we could start picking but Lerner was watching us, and it would be a quick pick, so he would have to come in for the trial. He said he couldn't and asked if we could do the trial or get someone to do it. We had been talking to a young trial attorney (Scott Zlotolow) about such possibilities, so while I was on the phone with the plaintiff's attorney, Diana ran into TAP and got Scott to come to the phone booth too.

We essentially did a phone booth conference call where I was on the phone with the attorney and relayed the facts of the case to Diana and Scott. The attorney's main instructions were "Diana should put a lot of Hispanics on the jury". While Diana was picking a jury on Rodriguez v Singh, Scott got the file from the attorney and prepared for the trial that would start the next morning. I went back to selecting a jury on a different case (where I actually started a trial and then the case settled).

After a jury was selected in Rodriguez v Singh, Diana reported back to TAP. The Clerk told her Judge Lerner would conduct the trial himself in the morning. We had seen this act before. It was going to be a rush trial in the TAP courtroom, designed as a lesson to the lawyers in TAP for why they should settle their cases. After my trial settled, I went to the TAP courtroom to watch Scott try Rodriguez v Singh. I whispered to Diana "Looks like 3 or 4 Hispanics on the jury. Great job!" The facts in Rodriguez v Singh were that Mr. Rodriguez was hit by a car while running across a street. He had a badly broken leg. The plaintiff's attorney and the insurance company agreed this was a $500,000 injury (this is how negligence lawyers talk), but they disagreed about liability (whose fault it was). That's what the trial was about: liability only. Most of the pre-trial talk was about whether Mr. Rodriguez had run out between parked cars, and whether Singh was speeding, or perhaps he should have seen the pedestrian. The jury would be asked to decide percentages of fault.

When the trial started, Judge Lerner rushed the testimony, so Rodriguez and Singh's testimony was done in an hour or so. There were no other witnesses. The lawyers made their closing arguments and the case went to the jury that afternoon. While the jury was out, we had more phone booth conference calls with the plaintiff's attorney, as he nervously grilled us about how the trial had gone. As the jury deliberated, as often happens, our side and the insurance company became more nervous. Scott had done a great job, getting a basic case presented to the jury despite Judge Lerner doing everything possible to foul him up. While there had been some testimony putting fault on the plaintiff, we did not think the verdict was going to be 100% against us. But you never really know.

At about 3:30 the jury sent a note they had reached a verdict. At that moment, Scott told me the insurance company had just offered $200,000. I called the plaintiff's attorney and gave him my assessment of the situation, which was "This is a total crapshoot. The jury is coming in. We should take the money!" He then asked, "What do you think the jury will say?"

I started yelling at him, "Listen, we all did what we were supposed to do, the jury is filing in and I need to know, are we taking the money?"

He thought for a moment and said, "Take it."

I ran in and told Scott to take it. He went up to Judge Lerner's clerk and said we had settled the case. Judge Lerner came out from the back and said, "You can do what you want, I am having the jury announce the verdict."

I said to Scott, "What should we do?"

Without hesitating, he took my legal pad and wrote the following: "Rodriguez v Singh – SETTLED for $200,000 notwithstanding jury verdict." He signed and handed it to the insurance company lawyer, who signed it as the jury was being seated to announce the verdict.

The jury announced a verdict finding the plaintiff 60% at fault and the defendant 40% at fault. Nobody needed to second guess anything. We had collectively gotten the case settled for exactly the right number!

I don't know whether the plaintiff's lawyer realized (or cared) what we had endured to get this result. Probably not. The whole situation was the talk of the Courthouse. Although we managed to get a good result, it sure was stressful and we knew our baby-sitting days were numbered.

Before too long, Diana and I made a better arrangement with Judge Lerner about the jury situation. He knew that when we appeared for pre-trial conferences, we were well prepared and tried in good faith to settle the cases. He also saw we were working hard and in a strange way helped move cases through the system. We also had a nice relationship with his court clerks and other court personnel, which was undoubtedly helpful.

The "arrangement" (never formalized but we all understood it) was we would stop the babysitting service and he would cut us (and our law firm clients) some slack when we appeared on pre-trial conferences. All he asked was that we come in prepared, tell him what was really going on, and work in ways that helped move the cases along. This was a great deal, since it got rid of the babysitting service we had come to detest, and greatly enhanced our standing and reputation for Queens per-diem work.

Some of my proudest per-diem moments were walking into a conference with Judge Lerner in a major injury, multi-party case, and after all the lawyers sat down, having the judge turn to me and say, "What's this all about?" I was always ready for this question and would give him a quick summary of the case and what I understood the parties' positions to be. It got the ball rolling, it saved time, and made it look like I was a "player". I wasn't really, but appearances do count.

All this activity culminated with my being featured on the front page of the *New York Law Journal* (It was the December 27, 1999 issue, but who can remember such things!). A *Law Journal* reporter had contacted me for a story about the per-diem business. She followed Diana and me around the courthouse, interviewed us, and wrote a very flattering story. A photographer took my picture on the courthouse steps, with the caption "Barry Seidel, the King of Queens." See Appendix E.

The *Law Journal* article was great for business, and also brought per-diem work into wider recognition. As the per-diem business grew, I added some additional modifications and improvements, such as:

- I was an early user of credit card payments for per-diem appearances. Most of my law firm clients paid promptly, but not all. The main use for credit cards in the per-diem world is to smoke out bad payers. The way I look at it, if a firm owes me more than $500 and won't make a credit card payment, I cut them off. This greatly improved collection turnaround rates. And, although I kind of hate to say this, it sent many of my worst payers to my newly emerging competitors.

- I offered volume discounts to certain clients. Although I did not initially intend to cover cases in Civil Court, per-diem really caught on with high volume collections law firms. The collection firms sue on lots of cases and have huge volume. Over the years, the collection firms became some of my biggest and best clients.

- I always made fair fee arrangements with my subcontractor attorneys. I had certain requirements for how to cover the appearances and tried to give my subs enough volume that I could ask them for a volume discount. I paid fairly and promptly. Per-diem coverage is a business, so I accepted that these issues would need to be thought about and addressed. Finding the right sub-contractors and creating a team culture was important.

- I experimented with offering various related services, most notably deposition coverage. Once things were busy, I couldn't do the depositions myself. I recruited attorneys who were willing to cover depositions, through my office, on behalf of my per-diem clients. I was in a great position to market this service, and for a few years I had tons of depositions. However, a big problem arose. I was paying most of the fee to the attorneys who did the depositions. On a $250 deposition, my share would be $25-$50. This was not bad for handling volume as a booking agent. Unfortunately, many of the firms took a long time to pay or made me chase them for the fees. Meanwhile, I was paying my lawyers within 30 days because it was the right thing to do. At one point this was such a big problem I made a new rule: Unless you were a primo payer, all depositions required a credit card payment. I even offered extra leeway by agreeing not to bill their card for sixty days. Guess what happened? The vast majority refused to agree to my terms, and my depositions business essentially stopped. This ended up being a good thing. My cynical side knows the unwillingness to pay by credit card showed these firm's true intentions. (It's not that they intended to stiff me, it's more that they wanted to pay when the case settled, which did not work for me when I had to pay my people.)

- I hired a person to handle the intake, set-up, and billing for the per-diem work. This cut into the profits, but there was no way I could handle the administrative side of per-diem work and still have time to run the rest of my law practice (Oh yeah, I still had that!) My approach was to hire a great person, pay well, and have their job description include both the per-diem prep and work with me on my regular cases.

- I paid attention to the many competitors who came into the per-diem business after my initial success. I made alliances with some, where we shared certain work and covered for each other. I tried to foster a non-cut-throat atmosphere among the per-diem "community" that developed in Queens. I discouraged client poaching, bad mouthing, and negativity. I encouraged information sharing (about particular judges or procedures, and about attorney-clients who were bad payers) and participation in the Queens Bar Association Court Committees, so we could advocate for ourselves. Over the years Bar Association participation has made a difference in how things run in Court. Of course, in the per-diem world there is the built-in paradox where "bad is good", because inconvenience and inefficiency in the court systems are bad for attorneys in practice but are good for lawyers doing per-diem work.

While I was growing the per-diem business, I still had about 150 negligence cases weighing on me. The cases were becoming more and more difficult. The insurance companies were becoming increasingly aggressive. It seemed like every company was defending every case to the hilt, in an effort to smack around the plaintiff's bar, and ultimately deter new cases. Cases that used to settle were being hit with motions to dismiss. These motions really put pressure on the plaintiff lawyers. I fell behind on some of these, and all the while, new potential clients were calling.

Every morning I was running around the courthouse doing the per-diem business, multi-tasking at frantic levels, all the while soaring on the success of my big marketing campaign and publicity from the *Law Journal* article. I wanted to bask in the glory, but I couldn't, because I knew I was cutting corners and handling the negligence cases sub-optimally.

When I got back from court after each day's per-diem cases, I was exhausted. The last thing I felt like doing was responding to some motion seeking to dismiss a back-injury case based on the "serious injury threshold." By that point these were cases I barely cared about.

I was caught in a bad cycle, with my frustration running high and my personal reserves running low. I knew it too, but didn't take action to correct things. I just worked harder and let my resentment and frustration increase.

Chapter 6

It All Caves In

On March 20, 2000, I walked up the steps to the second floor of Queens Supreme Court.

I felt fluttery in my chest and slightly dizzy. Another lawyer helped me over to a bench and I collapsed. Everybody except me seemed to realize I was having a heart attack. I was mostly thinking about how I was going to cover the sixteen cases I was scheduled to cover that morning.

I was taken to the closest hospital, Mary Immaculate, two blocks from the courthouse. I was given their basic heart attack protocol: a clot busting drug called TPA. This had been state of the art 15 years earlier. After two hours, a cardiologist told me the TPA wasn't working and that this was a "bad situation" where they weren't equipped to do anything more, so they were transferring me to Long Island Jewish. He said "You'll have a procedure as soon as you get there. Good luck."

I went in a fancy ambulance to LIJ, where I was taken directly to a room with a lot of equipment and a team waiting for me. I then had an angioplasty—they threaded a device through my wrist, up my arm and into the heart to unblock the blockage directly. They also put in a stent to keep the blocked artery open. I was awake the whole time and watched on a screen as my left anterior descending artery (a/k/a "the widowmaker") got unblocked. My heart attack was what doctors unscientifically call a "no risk factor" heart attack. I had no family history, was not overweight, not diabetic, and had normal cholesterol and blood pressure.

I was in the cardiac ICU for three days, including two days on an external heart pump, and in the hospital four more days after that. The heart attack did meaningful damage to my left ventricle. I was forty-three years old.

When I came home it was very clear I would not be working for some time (as it turned out, six months of no work, and another six months part-time only). Everyone told me to focus on getting better and not worry about the law practice. Knowing that I had great support from my wife and other family members, and my friends and fellow lawyers, made this part easier. I didn't worry much about the cases or the per-diem business because I wanted to make sure I survived. I had some disability insurance and a few bucks saved up, plus receivables coming in from the per-diem business, so I didn't have much concern about immediate finances.

I knew I would have to stay clear-headed and avoid making rash decisions. Being forced to take time away from work gave me space to better understand what had led to the heart attack.

Here's where I was when I had my blessed event: I was overwhelmed trying to keep up with the relentless pace of my work. The per-diem business was fast paced and kind of fun but facing the negligence cases was constantly stressful. I knew personal injury work was not a good fit for me, and I resented the pressure it caused. I also wanted to focus on important issues at home (our daughters were 14 and 7 then), but I was always felt the negligence cases gnawing at me. I surely had options, but I didn't see them.

While I was home recovering and considering my life choices, I was relieved not to have to actively work on the cases (heart attack is a universally accepted excuse) and was certainly not taking in any new ones. Whenever defendants tried to press me in court, Diana would get whatever adjournments I needed.

While I was away from the office, Diana continued growing her per-diem business, and covered most of my assigned appearances. Anything Diana couldn't handle I subbed out to other attorneys. Diana worked with Felicia to manage the administrative side of my per diem business, including intaking the work, setting it up for Court, making sure the appearances got covered, reporting and billing the results, and following up on collections. We made a fair arrangement, so she was properly paid while I received some income and kept my customer base intact.

After six months of cardiac rehabilitation, I visited the office. I was jarred by how shaky I felt. Everything seemed to move so quickly, and I had no desire to get involved. I knew I was not physically ready to go to court, or engage in any kind of law practice, and did not know if I ever would. I also knew if I went back to the same level of stress as I had before, I would have another heart attack and die. I'm not saying this to be dramatic. I knew I was in a weakened condition and could not go back to my old ways.

I sat and considered my options. One thought kept returning:

"If I were just a brain in a chair, with no physical presence, could I be a lawyer in practice?"

After meditating on this a bit, I knew the answer was yes. It could be done. It would take some thinking and restructuring and planning. It would involve winding down the negligence practice and delegating more of the per-diem work. It might involve exploring new practice areas that better suited me. It WAS possible.

Over the next few months I started putting some changes into place.

I didn't have to do much to the per diem biz: I brought in some more subcontractors. I tightened up the back office, which was easy because I was there every day. I saw myself as a manager and accepted that idea for as long as it might be needed.

While I was adjusting the per-diem model, I wound down the negligence cases. As necessary as it was, this was far from painless. It was more like negotiating a divorce that I knew was for the best. It took some persistence to get the cases settled, transferred to new counsel, or otherwise resolved. I spent my office time calling and settling the cases I could, referring some cases to colleagues, and preparing motions to withdraw from the most difficult situations.

I was relieved to be ending my negligence practice. Without new cases coming in, it took about a year. Daily calls to insurance companies settled quite a few cases and generated short-term cash flow. Oddly enough, in the year after my heart attack I posted the highest income of my career to that point.

After completing six months of formal cardiac rehabilitation, I continued physical conditioning at the same medical gym for another six months. Oftentimes, even after rehab, people who have had a heart attack are fearful of continuing to exercise without medical support nearby. That was me. Thankfully I had the good sense to take advantage of the gym's offer for continued services.

Heart attack rehab also included consultation with a psychologist. I worked with Dr. Robert Allan, who specialized in treating stress and anger related to cardiac issues. I did a few private sessions and then began attending weekly group therapy. I did this for about two years. The people in my cardiac group were at various stages of life and health. Everyone in the group had experienced a previous cardiac event (heart attack or bypass surgery), except one guy who hadn't, but knew he had stress and anger management issues.

Every week we all met and talked. I told my story, the group asked questions, then we discussed things. Everyone in the group had an interesting story, and I listened to them all. Dr. Allan offered guidance and insights as needed. For me, group therapy mostly involved listening to others, thinking and talking, and hearing myself give others advice I had not followed myself. It takes a while to recognize and alter ingrained thought processes. Regarding stress, I can sum up what I learned with Dr. Allan as follows:

Many people react to stress with anger. When anger responses become habitual as a first response to stress, there can be devastating physical consequences: one's blood chemistry changes, and plaques can become "sticky," causing heart attacks. Not only that, anger reactions tend to snowball into more outbursts. And, anger never actually solves any problems.

I learned that it is possible to disrupt the anger thought cycle and alter thought patterns, thereby improving reactions to stressors in our life. I went through and identified my numerous anger issues and triggers. Things that can trigger anger can be thought of as "anger hooks." Things like demanding situations and people, callousness from others, stupidity, unfairness, and time pressure. As we move through life, there are anger hooks dangling all around. We can bite at the lure and risk getting hooked, or see the hook for what it is and swim past.

But it's not enough to just avoid the hooks—it's important to simultaneously and proactively think, "What do I want?"

You'd be surprised how empowering this question is! The question fosters more direct, productive responses. It disrupts the ingrained, angry thought processes and forces you to consider better options than anger.

Being grateful to have survived, I tried to practice what I learned. It was/is an ongoing process.

In the spring of 2001, about a year after my heart attack, I made an arrangement with Diana to become partners on the per diem part of our practices. My role was to handle the office, billing and collections, business development, and everything other than the actual court appearances. She would handle most of the appearances, with the help of other per diem lawyers as needed. We essentially pooled our collective law firm clients, which totaled over 1000. I would make occasional appearances, subject to my ability, and I also kept a general private practice that she was not involved in.

We called ourselves Seidel & Gianturco ("the King and Queen of Queens") for a few years. It worked nicely, though we both soon realized that the per-diem business works much better if both partners are actually appearing. You can make some money subbing out the work, but the biggest profit is in actually appearing and not paying out. When you run a per diem service and make many of the appearances yourself, it's like giving yourself a well-paid salaried position at a company you own. When I was not making appearances, I wasn't really pulling my weight, and I knew it. We also realized that while a private practice needed an office and support staff, a strictly per-diem practice can work without those expenses.

After about two years, I felt mentally and physically able to make some court appearances. I started with just a few, to make sure I could still do it. I found that I could, though I made a conscious effort to manage myself better.

Seidel & Gianturco worked well and was fun, but after another year or so, for various reasons, Diana and I decided not to continue the partnership. We ended the partnership around 2004. The process was amicable and we resolved all our business without drama.

We're both still in the per-diem business in Queens and are still great friends. Not only am I eternally thankful to Diana for working with me in building the per-diem "industry" and then saving my business after the heart attack, I try to live by something she demonstrates every day, which is:

CHARACTER COUNTS!

As I wound down my negligence practice, I saw that the remnants of my practice would not be enough to live on. I had a nice following for per-diem work and knew I could make a living just running that, if I chose to.

I considered applying for a job at a law firm. I did some looking and put together a resume. I probably could have gotten a job, and some law firm would have gotten a good associate. But I never applied for a single job.

At that point, **I still wanted to have a law practice.** I just wanted to do it better.

Chapter 7

Probate and Estate Administration

Ah, but what kind of practice? I was healthy enough to work. I had twenty years of general practice experience, including concentrations in some specialties. As tough as negligence practice was, I learned a lot about negotiating, and about business, and about myself. My honest self-assessment was that I had never truly focused on any particular area of law. I had repeatedly reached competence, but each time stopped short of committing. Those experiences were not in vain. They got me to where I was. I knew I could make an informed and considered decision on what to do next.

Of the various areas of law I had encountered, only one really appealed to me: Probate and Estate Administration.

I wasn't interested in "estate planning" as a whole; rather, I liked the specific cases that were handled in the Surrogate's Court after someone had died.

This distinction was important to me. Estate planning for wealthy people means minimizing estate, gift, and income taxes for oneself and future generations, to the extent legally permissible. I had no interest in learning about that kind of legal work. I knew it would take much time and effort to learn it, and to keep up with constant changes in the law, and to catch up to the level of competitors who had decades of specialized experience. Probably the biggest deterrent, though, was I just wasn't a great match with this group of potential clients and their collective problems.

Please don't get me wrong. I have nothing against wealth or wealthy people. I respect people who have earned their fortunes, and I respect their right to protect their assets. I don't even have a problem with people who inherited their wealth. Luck is cool in my book, and they also have every right to receive legal advice.

Lawyers can do very well in estate planning, since they are offering a valuable service to people who need the service and can afford it. And, sheer demographics made this a growth field for years to come.

But spending my time giving such advice did not appeal to me. Money would not have changed that.

Related to estate planning for wealthy people is estate planning for middle class people—which should really be called: "Medicaid planning." This arises out of the monster lurking as every families' worst nightmare: That some family member will "end up in a nursing home," depleting their savings and assets, and leaving their family with nothing to inherit.

However, with a little planning and a few maneuvers, the person could become eligible for Medicaid, thereby sticking the government with the nursing home bill and preserving assets for their family to inherit.

For most middle-class people seeking help with "estate planning", that's the main issue. Many people do nothing and the nightmare happens; assets are wiped out by a nursing home. Or, without proper planning, even if the person gets on Medicaid, Medicaid can assert a lien after the person dies, wiping out everyone's inheritance. I have seen this scenario happen many times. It's tragic. As tragic as that is, it's even more sad that most folks could have spent a few bucks to avoid this tragedy entirely.

It's worth reiterating: Under our present system, middle class people should do estate planning, including Medicaid planning. It's stupid not to. There are many qualified elder law and estate planning attorneys who know how to do this. Most are highly qualified and creative, even brilliant. I have personally observed them collectively save *millions* of dollars for their clients.

However, for many of the same reasons I don't do estate planning, I chose not to be a lawyer who focuses on Medicaid planning. It took me a long time to learn that when you focus on something it becomes part of your identity. It becomes what you spend much of your time on. Doing (or not doing) areas of practice, however profitable they could become, is a decision worth deliberating. I couldn't see myself doing Medicaid planning.

Closely related to "estate planning" are basic wills. I always liked doing them and have done them for clients since I started. Basic wills avoid a different kind of tragedy than the Medicaid mess or big inheritance taxes. Basic wills avoid the tragedy where someone dies and their assets are not distributed as they would have wanted. Getting this right appeals to me.

I always kept the fees relatively low on regular wills because I wanted to do them. Besides the karma and the cash flow, there is business logic in doing wills at affordable prices, since they will often come back later as an estate. Of course, this is especially true when you treat clients well and they speak highly of you to their loved ones. When a surviving family member returns for estate help on a will you have done, it's not only a nice compliment, but a return on your earlier approach.

Early in my practice I bought a basic interactive wills program. It was easy to use and not expensive. With basic wills, we resolve the basic issues. Who gets what, who will be the executor, who will be the guardian for the kids, and anything else the client wants to address. I like it when people want to do specific things; make bequests to friends, make donations to charities, disinherit someone with colorful language, and the like. Regular wills are sufficient for many people. I like doing them so much, I make house calls if someone needs that.

But even with all that, you can't make a living on wills alone. I mentioned I was considering refocusing my practice on Probate & Estate Administration, not estate planning. So, you may be wondering—what is Probate & Estate Administration?

Probate & Estate Administration cases all start out the same way: "Somebody died, and then…"

In New York, "probate" means there is a will, "administration" means there isn't. Either way, the deceased person's assets are going somewhere. These cases all involve three key questions:

1. Is there a will or not?

2. Is the situation going to be friendly or unfriendly?

3. Are we being asked to represent the fiduciary (the person who will be acting on behalf of the estate) or someone affected by what the fiduciary is (or isn't) doing?

Although the stories all start out the same (*somebody died, and then...*), after that it's never the same. Sometimes it all falls into place, everybody is lovey-dovey, and it's just a matter of knowing what papers to file. Sometimes these cases become dysfunctional family feuds, with acrimony and bitterness that would humble the worst matrimonial case. If divorces involve anger, jealousy, and other toxic emotions, contested estates have that and more. There are often emotional issues that numerous family members (generally the children of an older person) have avoided discussing for many years. Frequently, financial decisions are being made as people sort through deep-seated emotional and psychological issues. I don't love these feuds, and starting out I had my share, but over time I moved away from the more bitter situations.

Estates are sometimes bitter, but even when they are bitter, at least at some point they end, and the surviving family members move on with their lives. Sometimes people realize this during the case and make peace. Sometimes not, but it's nice when it happens.

The bottom line is that as a lawyer you are finishing up a deceased person's affairs, and helping people move on. There is some professional and personal satisfaction in this.

When I decided to focus on this work, I only knew the fundamentals. I knew this area had its own set of laws and even its own court (in New York the cases are in Surrogate's Court.) I knew that sometimes the legal issues were complicated, but I knew managing them was within my abilities. It would take time to develop the expertise to be able to compete, but I knew there were fewer lawyers who focused on this work, compared with the thousands who work in personal injury and real estate. The competition was there, but it wasn't as crowded a field.

Having made the decision, I did a few things to bring my probate and estate skills to the next level.

I took CLE classes on Probate and Estate Administration. Sometimes it's a challenge to find interesting CLE classes, but in this situation I *really* focused on the material. As an aside, I tried a CLE on estate planning, which gave me basic knowledge of the lingo, but also helped confirm it was not for me. In the probate and estate classes, though, I was a sponge.

Whenever I was in Surrogate's Court, I paid careful attention, figured out which attorneys knew their stuff, and asked a lot of questions. As in the past, most were receptive to this.

I started writing blog posts about estate issues, and published them on "Blogger", a free service offered by Google. At that time this was a relatively new thing. I didn't really know how to set up Blogger and post to it, so I asked Felicia to set it up, which she did. Basically, when I learned something new and important in probate, I figured other generalists didn't know about it and would benefit from knowing. I wrote the articles and posts so that other lawyers, as well as potential clients, would get useful information. Over time, I began to promote the posts and articles on social media. I experimented on LinkedIn, Twitter, and Facebook, and adjusted my approach based on the responses.

I made sure to take the annual Queens County Bar Association CLE course on Surrogate's Court practice. Not only did I learn a lot, I made an effort to meet all the presenters, who were a "who's who" of Queens Estate lawyers.

As an attendee of this CLE, I was placed on the Queens Surrogate's list for Guardian-ad-Litem appointments. A Guardian-ad-Litem is appointed when the court determines there are "interested parties" who cannot speak for themselves. In Surrogate's Court this can be minors, incapacitated people, people whose whereabouts are unknown, and people who are incarcerated. When you are appointed you represent that person (or group of people) in the case. The person you represent is referred to as your "ward." It's like having a phantom client. You do some lawyering, but you are not consulting with or discussing fees with the client. If an estate is in court, there is generally money involved. Guardian-ad-Litem fees are determined by the Judge and are usually paid either from the estate or from the ward's share, at the end of the case.

There are many such situations and many such appointments. The fees were OK, but there was another great value in these appointments: I learned how to practice in Surrogate's Court.

I took the Guardian-ad-Litem appointments seriously. My approach was simple: "Always try to do a great job." The Guardian-ad-Litem work got me involved in cases with top lawyers. I paid careful attention and asked a lot of questions. Fairly soon, through this work I became known in Surrogate's Court by the lawyers, Court attorneys and the Judge.

Once probate work got a little busy, I hired a part-time associate who knew how to prepare Surrogate's Court papers. I invested in a Surrogate's Court document preparation program and learned how to use it. Actually, my associate learned how to use it. I mostly just knew what it did. As we got busier my associate asked if she could work full-time. I enthusiastically agreed, since I liked going to court better than preparing documents, and she prepared them way better than I could. She also handled much of the ongoing interactions with our clients.

To bring in new probate and estate cases I used a simple approach. I started by doing Google searches as if I were my ideal client. This required me to think about who my ideal clients and cases were. I thought about how my best potential clients would search for and hire an attorney after someone died. I typed in every query I could think of around the theme "a family member died and I have to figure out what to do in Queens Surrogate's Court." I studied the sites that came up. I knew some of the attorneys and called a few. I also looked at every page of every lawyer website that came up in my Google searches. I had no agenda other than to take it all in and think about what to do.

I then did some reading about website design, online marketing, and SEO (search engine optimization). I did not do this with a view towards doing any of these myself. But I knew that when I hired help, I would get better results if I understood what I wanted.

Before too long I launched my first probate website. I had an idea of what I wanted the site to do: provide useful information to potential clients who had the cases I would most want to do, and maximize the chance they would contact and retain me. Some attorneys are stingy with the information they put on a website. That seemed wrong-headed, so I did the opposite. I wanted the site to be detailed and informative and approachable. I knew that some clients would take free information and try to do things themselves to save money. So be it…those were not good clients for me to work with anyway. I wanted clients who would appreciate the information, ask good questions, and respect that I knew enough that my services had real value.

My first probate website was through Findlaw (a subsidiary of Westlaw.) I worked with one of their sales reps and discussed the strategy for the site. Findlaw itself has legal information and hosts many lawyer websites. Those things were OK with me, but I sensed that their main value would be in having my site come up on page one of Google searches from my ideal clients.

I appreciated that Findlaw offered to handle just about everything (site design, securing names, and SEO). However, they respected that I wanted to do most of the writing myself. I kept a little of their "website-speak" on the site but spent some quality time writing about the various probate scenarios in a conversational, practical tone.

Over time, I learned and incorporated some important principles of effective online marketing—basically: you need to clearly identify your ideal types of clients, refine how you define yourself, and keep refining both your ideal client profile and your own online identity, all the while posting useful content for such clients.

I called the Findlaw site www.queensprobate.com. I was willing to handle cases outside Queens County, but all other things being equal, I preferred the home Court. As an aside, the site generated plenty of estate matters in the surrounding counties too, though by far most of the inquiries were on Queens cases.

Writing the website copy took some time and effort but was well worth it. My initial financial commitment to the site was one-year for approximately $300 per month. When I started the site, I used my tried and true mathematical calculations, which were if the site cost me $3,600 for the year, I would need one decent case to break even. The week the site went live I was retained on several cases, had more than paid for the site for a year, and found myself quickly busy with new matters. New clients seemed to connect with the tone of the site, and they often told me so.

I did get some crazy people and some problematic situations, but even the worst of those taught me valuable lessons. At that point in my career, I was a quick study when it came to figuring out what worked and what didn't, and how to adjust. Over time I narrowed the types of cases and clients I'd accept, and adjusted my online presence to reflect those adjustments.

Some of the most profitable new matters were cases where the "Public Administrator" was one of the other parties. The Public Administrator is involved in cases where there is nobody in a position to act on behalf of an estate. Once they are involved, they notify people who have a legal interest in the Estate. These cases happen fairly often, so I wrote about Public Administrator cases on the website.

When people who had an interest in an estate were served with papers from the Public Administrator, very often they Googled "Public Administrator" and found my website with its explanations of Public Administrator cases. This brought me even better cases, especially so-called "kinship" cases. These are cases where distant relatives may be inheriting, but they have to prove their kinship before the Public Administrator can receive a court order to pay them. These cases are fun, interesting, and generally profitable, so I wrote on the site about various kinship scenarios. When I started doing probate and estate work, I wasn't even aware of kinship cases. Before long, I had handled a few and was writing about them with some level of expertise.

Many kinship cases involve the inheritance rights of first cousins, where they are the closest surviving family members and there is no will. I titled an entire section on the site "Cousin Cases" and specifically wrote about such cases. Before long, when I did online searches for "first cousin and Public Administrator," my site was coming up first. One day the counsel to the Queens Public Administrator told me that if someone Googled just "Queens Public Administrator," my site came up ahead of theirs!

Fairly often, I'd receive calls from out-of-state (and foreign country) attorneys who had clients with a New York estate situation and needed a New York attorney to handle the case. In these scenarios, the attorney had simply Googled "New York probate attorney" and found my site. It felt good having expertise and being recognized for it.

Although I did not initially realize it, probate work also fit my peer and age group. I could speak from first-hand experience and empathize with clients who had lost a close family member. Some lawyers might be uncomfortable talking about death and the legal aftermath, but I never was. Whether untangling complicated situations, or finding creative solutions, or negotiating the resolutions of family feuds, I knew I was doing some good by finishing up the affairs of someone's life, and I found the work to be quite satisfying.

Estate work often requires knowledge of other legal areas. Having worked in general practice, landlord/tenant, real estate, litigation, negligence, and "per-diem" areas, my experiences all came into play.

If an estate has Landlord/Tenant questions, I am familiar with the issues. If an estate needs to sell real estate, I can do it. If the deceased person had a pending negligence case when they died, I know what to do. And even when I don't know what to do, I know (or can find) someone who does.

Another thing that built my confidence and expanded my skills was being involved in a few particularly difficult cases. Here's the story of one of them...

My Client Made a Big Mistake – So I figured Out What To Do

My client's prior lawyer had gotten him appointed Administrator of an Estate, filing papers as if he were a nephew of the deceased person, when in fact he was only a cousin. It was a mistake, though I could understand how it happened. The client's Aunt had a lot of money and died, so her daughter had the right to inherit it all. However, she died fairly soon after her Mom, and had not collected any of the money. My client and his lawyer viewed this as the Aunt's money, but filed papers in the daughter's estate as if he and his siblings were nieces and nephews. In fact, they were only first cousins to the person who was entitled to the money (the daughter), and not the only ones!

The client was appointed Administrator and collected several hundred thousand dollars and distributed it to his siblings. The lawyer should have realized his client's status, which was a mistake, but an even bigger mistake was telling the client he could pay out what he had collected. After the client distributed what he had collected, a new lawyer appeared in the case on behalf of 42 additional first cousins. They were cousins of the daughter, same as my client and his siblings. If my client and his group had been inheriting from the Aunt, they would have been the only ones. But their inheritance was legally through their first cousin. So, there were 48 heirs in all. My client, his 5 siblings, and the other 42 cousins.

When the lawyer for the other cousins informed the Court what had happened, my client's appointment as Administrator was revoked, and the Public Administrator was appointed instead. After they collected the rest of the money (which was a substantial amount), they sued my client to get back the hundreds of thousands he had paid out to his siblings. Unfortunately, they had all spent the money, so my client was on the hook for it all.

The client found my website through a Google search that included "Queens Public Administrator." I know this because I asked him.

I thought his lawyer had made a mistake by directing him to pay out when he did, so I wrote to the lawyer, explained the problem, and asked if he had legal malpractice insurance. He did.

I initially asked the Surrogate's Court to allow me to bring the legal malpractice case as part of the Surrogate's Court proceedings. I researched whether this was allowed and argued that the Court had the discretion to accept the case, and that they should. The Surrogate and the Public Administrator's lawyers were dismissive of this (actually– they laughed at the idea). So, I represented my client in the Surrogate's Court case, knowing that we would ultimately lose and my client would be ordered to pay the Estate all the money he had paid out. However, the whole time I kept the prior lawyer's malpractice carrier (and the lawyer they had assigned) apprised of the case. They knew that if my client got hammered, they were going to get hammered in the malpractice case I had started (and then essentially put on hold) in Supreme Court.

The Surrogate's Court case went on for over a year. There were depositions and motions and conferences. At the last pre-trial conference before the Surrogate's Court case was going to trial, the Surrogate (which is what we call the Judge in Surrogate's Court) saw the malpractice defense lawyer sitting in the front row observing the conference. The Judge asked him why he was there. When he explained it, the Judge invited him to participate in the conference "to see if we could reach a global resolution".

Which we then did.

I can't say I knew from the outset this was going to happen, but I suspected it. I defended the Surrogate's Court case with a legal malpractice case all teed up against the prior attorney. It was a lot of work, but I was focused on things and had a plan.

I can't say it felt good because admittedly, it was a lot was a lot to think about over a pretty long time.

But I CAN say that the Surrogate and the Public Administrator's attorneys seemed to respect me a lot more after they realized what I had orchestrated. The prior attorney's legal malpractice carrier stepped forward and paid the Estate for the funds my client had incorrectly paid out.

It really helps to earn credibility in court and among adversaries. After that case was settled and over, I felt like I had that.

I've been involved in some complicated Surrogate's Court cases and trials. I had to up my skills and prepare well. Funny thing, very often when you do this the cases settle. The prep and reputation make the settlement results a lot better. This was true in negligence, and of course is true in estate litigation and every aspect of law practice.

As I continued in the probate and estate field, I refined the types of cases I preferred. Sometimes we have to do things we don't like, learn some lessons, and adjust our standards. I admit, there were some difficult, unpleasant estate cases that I regretted accepting. But I soon realized I had to reject those kinds of matters and focus on cases I actually liked.

It helped to be very clear in defining the kinds of cases I would accept going forward—and for me, those cases were:

- probating wills when people are in agreement.
- appointing Administrators when there is no will, and then guiding the Administrator through the estate process.
- Guardian-ad-Litem appointments.
- Kinship cases.
- Ancillary probate cases. These occur when an estate is initially handled in another state or a foreign country. If there is New York property, someone needs to be appointed in New York. These cases involve gaining a working knowledge of Estate work in other States or countries and interacting with lawyers from those places. I find these cases fascinating—but of course, to each his own!

It's nice to practice confidently. It's nice to know a lot but learn something new every day. It's nice to be well paid and know your work and skill and experience are recognized and valued.

While building the probate and estate practice, I also kept the per-diem business. For the sake of my mental and physical health, I made a few adjustments.

I converted the per-diem business to a model where a larger portion of the court appearances were delegated to other lawyers. I still appeared regularly, but in a more controlled way. However, I didn't simply "farm out" the appearances. I hired, trained, and supervised the lawyers and my office staff. I wanted my name to be associated with quality appearances, great back office service, and prompt reporting. I did not think most of my law firm clients required that I make every appearance myself, and for the most part, this was true. If the clients really needed me personally, I made the appearance.

By not making all the appearances myself, I made less money at per-diem work than the lawyers who do everything themselves. I also delegated most of the back-office functions to my outstanding assistant. She does the intake and set-up and reporting better than me, and the trade-off of expenses versus lifestyle is well worth it.

With all that, relative to the work I do, the per-diem business was/is still profitable. Most of the time, making the appearances is kind of fun. For me, the per-diem practice is like running a business while also having a law practice.

Chapter 8

Still Evolving – What I Do Now

As you've seen, I shifted my law practice focus several times. I am still practicing and as far as I can tell, still learning and improving. I suppose that's why we call it a "practice". We work at it until we get it right, knowing of course that we never will. We simply keep adapting.

I currently maintain both my per-diem business and my probate & estate administration practice. I strive to maintain the right balance.

I pay attention to the per-diem business climate, where there are many issues if one chooses to look. When big changes were made in the workings of Queens Supreme Court, I analyzed what was needed and made some new alliances and arrangements to suit the changes. I also wrote articles about the changes and published them online, mostly on LinkedIn. Of course, I also put the LinkedIn articles out there on Twitter, Facebook and Instagram. Every time I try something new on social media, I learn something.

I treat per-diem like a business and pay attention to the three elements of any business, which are:

- Bringing in new work.
- Doing the work well.
- Paying attention to finances.

With a few caveats, doing the actual per-diem appearances is not that difficult. The caveats are:

- You need to know if an appearance is actually appropriate for a per-diem attorney. Sometimes you have to reject or refer these out. Sometimes I will agree to do an appearance but will issue a disclaimer, like "you have asked me to seek an adjournment which we may not be able to get under the circumstances."

- You need to be able to determine when there is too much on the plate on any particular day. In those situations, I bring in help, but I am careful about who I work with and how I manage things.

- A sense of camaraderie and community with other per-diem attorneys is very helpful. This is a business, but we end up being on lots of cases together. It is basically understood that while we have to carry out our clients' instructions, we don't seek to hurt each other. We also don't generally poach each other's clients. I say generally because there are situations where law firm clients decide to change per-diems. That's part of any business, but overt soliciting is frowned upon.

- You have to know how to make a "per-diem game plan" and execute it. To handle volume (and the only way to make money at per-diem is with volume) you need to have or develop the per-diem multi-tasking gene. Part of the game plan is knowing which appearances are "check-ins" and which are a "calendar call." Check-ins are much easier. You also need to know your adversaries and the court clerks. You need to know the various deadlines and default times. And, you need to have (or get) good instructions from the attorneys who hire you.

For my probate & estate administration practice, it took some time to find the right model. Eventually I realized I was saying yes on too many contested matters. Those involved toxicity and dysfunctionality and were stressful. So, I started using a new standard for accepting new matters, which is: "If it's not a *hell-yeah*, it's a *no*." (with credit and appreciation to Derek Sivers, who said this on a Tim Ferris podcast.)

I needed to figure out whether, if I looked past the more stressful cases, there was still enough work out there to have a healthy business going forward. Once I confirmed that there was, I looked for the way to bring in those kinds of clients. Anyway, that's been the recent game plan.

The Other Things I Do Now –

This book is my next evolution.

I've always done a bit of writing, speaking, teaching and consulting about law practice.

My plan is to evolve to where I spend more time ("as much as possible" seems about right) helping other lawyers who are looking at the entrepreneurial path.

To any students, law students, lawyers, and entrepreneurs, I say…

"You cannot totally control where the ship of your life will sail, but you *CAN* steer!"

Chapter 9

Thoughts on Practicing Law and Starting a Solo Law Practice Today

Could someone actually open a practice right out of law school today? Can lawyers who work at law firms start their own practices today?

YES to both questions! This is not to say it would be (or ever was) easy. Here are just a few reasons why starting and growing a law practice has become more feasible:

- A lawyer can quickly create a real presence for a legal niche, using websites and social media.

- Along the same lines, lawyers can (and should) develop focused expertise on niche areas. The amount of readily available resources, and opportunities to learn fields of law quickly, are vast and ever-increasing.

- Technological advances have driven expenses and over-head WAY down from where it used to be.

- There are new areas of practice emerging every day.

- Contrary to what many lawyers think, the proliferation of non-lawyer sites like LegalZoom does not mean that law-yers cannot serve regular folks and their need for basic legal services. On the contrary, the fact that LegalZoom is spending millions to market to these clients only shows the demand. As lawyers we can serve these clients WAY better than do-it-yourself forms, IF we price our services right, work efficiently, and make sure clients know we are doing this.

I also note that if you have a part-time job and one client, *you are already in practice*. If you have a job where bringing in business is encouraged, and you can participate in the fees, *you are in practice*. Many firms are agreeable to fee sharing arrangements and greatly respect young lawyers who are entrepreneurial and can bring in business.

Common sense tells me there are areas of practice that are sure to grow. I dare say lawyers who have any modicum of expertise in ANY particular legal field have a highly marketable skill. A few fields jump out at me, and I will share them, but I do think the possibilities are infinite.

Immigration is a big one, and of course clients with immigration issues invariably have other legal needs. Oftentimes, if you were the immigration attorney, you are the point person for all future legal questions. This is an example of why, whatever field you enter, you should also develop your network of related lawyers.

Elder law is another one. This is simply demographics.

IP and technology. Legal issues exist across the board. If you have valuable legal knowledge and treat your law practice like a business, you can and should compete for this work. Oh, and when you add in the international aspect of this, it's mind-boggling.

There are obviously many more. I hope you are looking for and finding them!

EPILOGUE:

What Have I Learned?

Law practice, business and life are all related and intertwined. All we can do is pay attention to the MANY decisions we get to make, and then try to improve our decisions and actions. Here are a few brief observations that I hope will be helpful, or at least thought provoking.

- When you do things, things happen!!!!
- Pay attention to results.
- Take care of your physical and mental health....proactively.
- Hire (and work with) people whose skills exceed yours.
- Money is important and has emotional components. Be aware. It's a useful way to measure certain things, but it diminishes in stature compared to being true to yourself.
- If your gut and your brain tell you that money is your primary motivation for doing something, at the very least step back and think it over.
- If something is broken, fix it before you become broken.
- We always have the ability to refine how we define ourselves. It's a decision we get to make repeatedly.
- Be curious, ask questions.
- There is no substitute for character and integrity.

- A meditative mind is worth cultivating. It leads to better decisions.
- Things do not always go as planned, but the only real failure is failing to learn.

APPENDICES

Appendix A – Essential Guide to Letter Writing

All business letters can be successfully composed following a 3 step outline, as follows:

1. Identify yourself and the other players. You can never go wrong starting a letter with "I am the attorney for…." and saying as much as needed so the recipient knows who you are.

2. State the facts or the situation. This is the essence of good letter writing. I will sometimes start with phrases like "It is my understanding that…." or "My client has informed me that…" Then you lay out the current situation. If you can't state this clearly, or if you don't yet know enough to explain your current knowledge, get more information and hold off the letter until you have this. If part of the facts are that you don't have complete information, you can usually state this.

3. State what you want or what actions will be upcoming. Generally, if you have stated the facts in an organized way, the recipient has a sense of where you are going. In this section you are usually suggesting that the recipient do something by a certain time. Very often this involves the recipient (or their attorney) contacting you back. Every

situation is a bit different, but there should be some "call to action" or stated consequence for inaction.

Appendix B - Joe Milner's current law firm website https://www.fmltlaw.com/our-firm/attorney-profiles/joe-milner/

Appendix C – The contingency tripod of legal liability, damages, collectability….. When a lawyer evaluates a case for a possible contingency fee, it's like a three-legged stool. If one of the three legs is weak (or not there) the stool would fall down, and you can't/shouldn't take the case.

The first leg is "liability". There has to be some legal basis for the claim. Sometimes people think that just because someone got hurt pretty bad, it must be a case. But there has to be a legal theory for a case. When someone falls on someone else's property, in and of itself there is no legal basis for liability. Some type of "negligence" has to be proven. Sometimes you look at the facts and it's either not there or not strong.

The second leg is "damages". In a case involving money, like a debt collection case, how much is involved? In an injury case, how serious are the injuries. A great liability case without meaningful injuries is not going to be worth it. Most negligence lawyers look at the damages aspect first. A lawyer will be more willing to consider a questionable liability case if the damages are large. It's a gamble, but these cases are gambles for insurance companies too, so such cases (big damages and questionable liability) may have value. As noted earlier, these are business decisions we get to make repeatedly.

The third leg is "collectability". This usually means "how much insurance is there?" but it also applies in litigation involving claims for money. If a case has good liability and is for a lot of money, it's not a good contingency case (for the lawyer) if the defendant has no assets. Sometimes this is a factor to investigate, but to be sure, if there is nothing to collect the contingency tripod falls.

Appendix D – Queens Court Appearances rolodex card

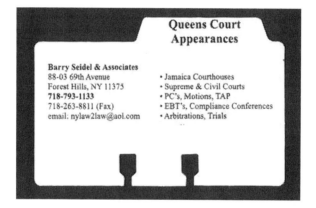

Appendix E – "The King of Queens"

New York Law Journal

SERVING THE LEGAL PROFESSION SINCE 1888

Web address: http://www...

VOLUME 222—NO. 123   NEW YORK, MONDAY, DECEMBER 27, 1999   PRICE $3.00

Solo Converts Courthouse Frustrations Into Profits

BY VICTORIA RIVKIN

PHOTOGRAPH BY RICK KOPSTEIN

THE KING OF QUEENS: Lawyer Barry Seidel outside Queens Supreme Court, Jamaica.

IT IS 9 A.M. on any given motion day at the Queens Supreme Courthouse in Jamaica, and swarms of lawyers shuffle in to stake out their posts in different court parts for a preliminary conference, a compliance conference or to file a motion. By first and second call, courtrooms fill up with lawyers lounging around for hours waiting to adjourn or move their cases, their expressions growing more and more exasperated as the clock ticks away.

An uncanny contrast to these frustrated souls is a group of lawyers who learned to turn their colleagues' frustration into their own profit.

One such lawyer, Barry Seidel, over the last seven years has built up a lucrative and busy practice handling preliminary and compliance conferences, motions, trial assignment parts and filings for other lawyers in Jamaica's courthouses.

With Mr. Seidel's services, lawyers are spared hours of waiting for a few-minute session with a law secretary or a clerk. They can remain in the office working on other matters, and for a mere $75, on the average, Mr. Seidel will appear in court for them.

On the average motion day, Mr. Seidel, 42, handles roughly 20 matters. A typical motion day calls for 50-75 motions in front of each judge, all scheduled at the same time, he explained. In order to grow his business, Mr. Seidel employs several contract attorneys to work with him.

At 9:15 a.m., Mr. Seidel and his band of lawyers take off in a mad dash through the Jamaica courthouse to cover the daily load of matters in multiple courtrooms on any one of its seven floors. Mr. Seidel races from one courtroom to the next, often foregoing the overcrowded elevators in favor of sprinting up and down the steps, intermittently responding to calls on his beeper from a

lawyer/client asking for help in covering a matter that was called by a clerk an hour ago. Not quite an Olympic quality relay squad, but close, the team has worked out a system for not missing cases and helping each other in times of need.

"I don't sit down too often," said Mr. Seidel, who does not take a break until the early afternoon. "Basically, some-

Continued on page 5, column 1

how, we always land on our feet," he said.

Over the last five years, Mr. Seidel has covered matters for 475 different law firms and he claims to represent about 100 firms on a regular basis. Most cases involve plaintiffs' personal injury matters, but he also handles work for defendants and some insurance companies.

Letter Campaign

Mr. Seidel got his business off the ground by mailing letters to more than one thousand lawyers describing himself, his work arrangements and his fees. The letter campaign proved successful, but Mr. Seidel is still using mailings and handing out his card to the exasperated lawyers waiting for a clerk to call their cases.

Mr. Seidel, a talkative Queens native, attributes his success to working in one county. "I strongly believe that in order to succeed in per diem work you have to concentrate in one county. The economics are against you if you are trying to run around between different counties," he said. "The travel, the unfamiliarity and the waiting will kill you," he added.

Although he is not the first to start this practice, he realized early on in his solo career that there is a great need for such services. "It works because of a basic business truth: success is finding and filling a demand in the marketplace," said Mr. Seidel.

He is not alone in realizing the profitability of such a business.

Diana C. Gianturco also runs a similar full-time business in Queens, and on occasion, works with Mr. Seidel.

Mr. Seidel, for example, said he nets about $750-1,000 per day, while Ms. Gianturco said she nets on the average $500 per day.

The "lack of continual involvement with the file" is what Ms. Gianturco said drew her to this work and away from her own cases. "I'm like a soldier in battle. I love being able to move the case through the system," she said.

She is so happy with the per diem practice that she has mostly given up taking her own cases. "I never anticipated a whole practice based on per diem. I like per diem work better because you don't live with the case for five years," she said.

But Mr. Seidel still takes his own cases, which he handles in the afternoons. "I like having lawyers as clients because we both know what the other is talking about, we are both busy so we get right to the point and we almost never have fee disputes," said Mr. Seidel.

ACKNOWLEDGEMENTS

Over the years I have been fortunate to interact with literally thousands of clients, lawyers, judges, employees, court people, friends and family. It's a big part of what lawyers do.

To my clients I wish to say thank you for the opportunity to help you. I hope I was worthy of your confidence and that you know I gave my best efforts. As much as law practice is a business, very often it is also about relationships. To those clients where we had that, and especially where you came to consider me "your lawyer"....THANK YOU.

I included some lawyers in this book by name, including Joe Milner, Charles Knox LaSister, Larry Litwack, Paul Weitz, Harvey Weitz, Diana Gianturco and Scott Zlotolow. In various ways you were part of my story, and I am happy to acknowledge and say thank you, both here and in the text.

Certain lawyers really helped me with advice and encouragement throughout my career. A few who I wish to specifically acknowledge are Jack Babchik, Susan Cartier-Liebel, John Chapman, Phil Durst, Stephen Fink, David Karel, Paul Kerson, Anthony Montiglio, Joseph Neiman, Greg Newman, James Pagano, Murray Singer, Gerard Sweeney and Jay Youngdahl.

A special note of thanks to the late Gerald M. Singer, Esq. As noted in the book, he was an attorney in Los Angeles who wrote *How to Go Directly Into Solo Law Practice (Without Missing A*

Meal). I followed his basic plan and referred to his book often. I still have my original copy and I still refer to it. Back in the 80's I wrote to him and kept the encouraging handwritten note he sent in response. I searched for him when I started this book and found out that he passed away in 2011 at the age of 90. I do not know how many other attorneys were inspired by his book, though I am sure I was not the only one. All I can say to Mr. Singer is a big THANK YOU!

In the Queens courts I have worked with many outstanding "per-diem" lawyers, including but not limited to Mohammed Baig, Jeff Boyar, Danielle Caminiti, Norman Chan, Ed Cherubin, Jeremy Davis, Eileen Donovan, Melba Feliberty, Fania Jean, Manny Kossaris, Evelina Luzhansky, Swati Mantione, Ed Marion, Gary Muraca, George Nicholas, Nirav Shah, Stavros Skenderis, Stacy Spodick, Michael Stea and Leonard Ziegler. We are truly part of a "community". Thank you all for doing what you do and for making it fun to come to court in Jamaica and Long Island City.

I've had quite a few law clerks and students work for me, some of whom are referenced indirectly in the text. Not only did I appreciate your work, I appreciated the opportunity to impart whatever experience and wisdom I could. With that in mind, thank you to Heather Capell, Leigh Cheng, Bernadette Dono, Richard Getzel, Joe Liberta, Sharmila Singh and Neil Tomeo.

I have appeared in front of many Judges in many courts. Sometimes it's an awkward relationship because we are all doing our jobs. No matter what though, I appreciate the great public service provided by all the Judges. It would not be appropriate for me to acknowledge any currently sitting Judge, as I am still in practice. To all of you I will simply say a collective "thank you", both as a lawyer and a citizen.

I do wish to specifically acknowledge a few Judges who are no longer sitting, and who had an impact on my career. The late Justice Alfred Lerner is referenced specifically in the book. I appreciated that he did his job so well, and at the same time respected me and what I was doing. Thankfully, we found ways to make things work.

The late Justice Joseph Risi, Sr. is referenced indirectly in the text as the Judge in Civil Court who cut me some slack when I needed it. After he retired I told him just how much I appreciated his kindness, and now I am happy to say it publicly.

Recently retired Justice Jeremy Weinstein was the Administrative Judge in Queens for many years while I practiced as a per-diem lawyer. Your Honor - Thank you for many years of service and for respecting input and suggestions from me and my lawyer colleagues. And of course, your sense of humor (both in Court and out) made some difficult work much easier.

Thank you also to retired Surrogate Judge Robert Nahman. He appointed me as Guardian-ad-Litem numerous times when I was breaking into probate practice. This was the single greatest factor in my learning how to practice in Surrogate's Court, for which I am thankful.

I have had two long standing employees, who are both referenced in the book, though not by name. I want to acknowledge them here.

My associate Audrey Frankel enabled me to start, grow and build my probate practice. We have discussed and strategized about hundreds of probate matters, made plans on every one of them, and professionally served our clients' interests. Discussing the cases and working together has not only made us both better lawyers, it enabled me to find joy in my professional work, for which I am eternally grateful.

My extraordinary assistant/paralegal Clarizza Pereira runs my per-diem practice AND supports Audrey and I in every aspect of the rest of my practice. My clients all know what a great job she does, and if I told her every time they tell me (which is often) we'd never get any work done. She has supported me through several evolutions, including the current ones. I could not have written this book without her help. Thank you for everything you do!!!

I have some good friends who have also helped me personally and professionally. This is sometimes with advice, sometimes with encouragement or constructive criticism, and sometimes by simply listening. Thank you then to:

Mitch Applebaum (the title salesman who cold-called me and then became my good friend), and to

Joel & Susan Brenner, who always have the knack for listening and providing just the advice I need, and to

Lorili Henry, for personal and spiritual guidance, and to

Glenn Darnell, for friendship and support through thick and thin, and to,

Marla and Jorge Cornejo, for showing me first-hand that one can accomplish much, be a friend to many, and also have fun times, and to

My mother-in-law Beverly Sacks, for supporting me and my family in every way and also for demonstrating the value in adapting to the times, and to

My brother, Brian Seidel, who understands that a brother who is also a friend is invaluable.

My mother Rita Seidel and my father Manny Seidel enabled me to become who I am. I miss them every day, but I appreciate that writing this book helped me know myself better, and more fully understand how much they each meant to me.

I always viewed my Mom as "creative" (which she surely was) and myself as not so much. Besides being an artist, she was creative in always setting her own agenda and following her own path. She taught me this by example and I put it into practice, something I only recently realized.

I used to think that the main lesson I learned from my Dad was the concept of "being a mensch". This was so, but he also inadvertently inspired me to write this book. This happened when he was about 80. He called to wish me a happy birthday, but then apologized for never sending me a birthday card because "it's just not something I do". I pointed out that I had written a blog piece called "Power of Yet", and that maybe he just hadn't sent a card, yet. He asked me to send him the piece, which I did, and then I forgot about it. The next year he sent me a great card (pictures of boys paying baseball with their father) and wrote on it "This card reminds me of the best times in our lives. YET is NOW!"

I only started writing this book in earnest after getting that card. It took awhile, and for many years I told people "I'm writing a book, which isn't quite ready, yet."

Dad – Yet IS now.

My daughters Emilie and Rebecca inspired me to always keep trying, even when things were rough. I am thankful that I figured out how to "live to tell about it" so I can tell you how proud I am of you both, and how thankful I am to be able to say it.

My wife Felicia is mentioned in the text a few times, in the context of her entrepreneurial approach and computer/business skills. To the extent that this memoir about law practice shows the interplay between business and life, I have not done her justice. She overflows with patience, wisdom, endurance, creativity and light.

Thank you my love for traveling with me through it all.